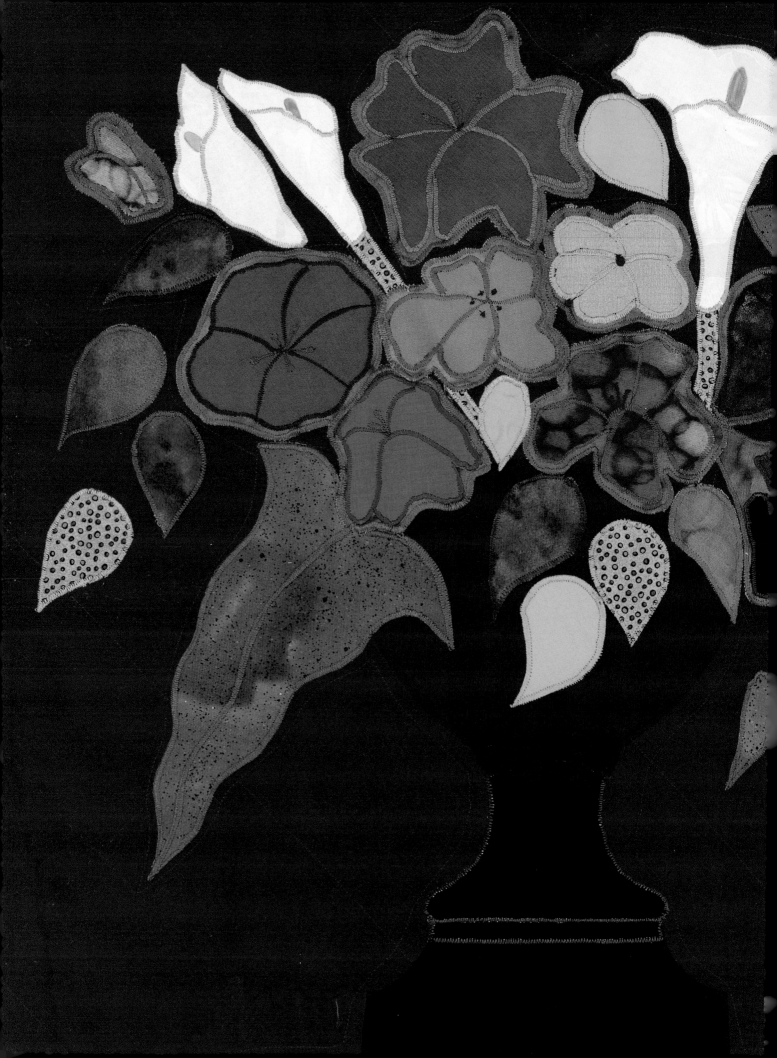

# ART & INSPIRATIONS

## Yvonne Porcella

C&T PUBLISHING

Editor: Annie Nelson
Technical Editor: Sally Loss Lanzarotti
Copyeditor: Judith M. Moretz
Book Design: Lesley Gasparetti
Front and Back Cover Design: Micaela Carr
Front Cover: *Still Life With Five Oranges*, 36" x 28", 1995

**Library of Congress Cataloging-in-Publication Data**
Porcella, Yvonne.
    Yvonne Porcella: art & inspirations/Yvonne Porcella.
            p.          cm.
    Includes bibliographical references and index.
    ISBN 1-57120-056-8 (hardcover).—ISBN 1-57120-050-9 (pbk.)
    1. Textile crafts.  2. Quilting.  3. Quilted goods.  4. Fancy work.  5. Wearable art.  I. Title.
TT699.P67     1998
746.46—dc21                                    98-4700
                                               CIP

Published by C&T Publishing, Inc.
P.O. Box 1456
Lafayette, California 94549

Printed in Hong Kong
10    9    8    7    6    5    4    3    2    1

# table of contents

# acknowledgments

I want to thank the staff at C&T Publishing for helping in the development of this publication, from guiding the manuscript through each stage to completion, and then into the marketing arena. Annie Nelson did a superb job as editor, helping me interpret my career and translate it into a beautiful book. Diane Pedersen generously offered her quiet strength and direction from the beginning of this project. Sharon Risedorph has photographed my quilts since 1985, and her talent always makes my work look so beautiful. Lesley Gasparetti, who worked on *Six Color World*, understands just what is needed to design a book around my words and photographs.

The special people in my life are the members of my family, both the living and those who have passed on. I have so many wonderful memories of my family —this book only touches a small part of them. Friends have also played a large part in my success through their support and enthusiasm for my work.

For 40 years, my husband Bob's encouragement has allowed me to pursue my art. For it is my art which has surfaced from deep within me. I did not set out upon this journey deliberately, but rather, it took me by the hand and led me.

Our four children, Stephen, Suzanne, Gregory, and Donald; their respective spouses, Sandy, Tim, and Madhu; and our grandchildren, Tori, Angelo, Nick, Vince, Eric, Mikey, Mimi, Elie, Sarina, Robbie, and Monique have increased both the size and love of our family, and that gives us great joy.

In 1980, a family friend, Monsignor William P. Kennedy, gave me a small book by M. B. Goffstein, entitled *An Artist*. Through the years I have enjoyed rereading passages from that book; one of my favorites reads as follows: "An artist is like God, but small."

In 1963 I made my first quilt as a special gift. There is no photograph or documentation of it, but I remember it well. I had seen a quilt in a magazine and the design inspired me to attempt to make one myself. I pieced a quilt top in a similar style and then called my mother to ask if she could help me with the finishing. The gift was due in two weeks. Her immediate response was that it takes a lifetime to make a quilt, but she agreed to help anyway. We used the living room floor to layer the quilt top over a flannel sheet (the batting), and a bed sheet (the backing), and we tied the layers together with crochet cotton thread. Much to mother's amazement, we managed to meet the deadline.

Knitting, crochet, embroidery, and sewing were the talents possessed by the women in my family. Quilting was not. I remember most the handmade clothes, the embroidered pillowcases, and the beautiful handknit sweaters. My mother also made bedspreads for each of her young daughters. The spreads featured an appliquéd top with a bed sheet as the backing and a flannel sheet as the batting. They were tied to hold them together.

"Life experience" best describes my artistic education. My creative energy developed one step at a time—each completed project has logically flowed into the next. I notice a progression of color and design, from the earliest years when I was a weaver and maker of wearable art, to my present interest in art quilts. Certain artistic elements of color and imagery transcend my work and have been repeated or enhanced over a thirty-year period.

When I was asked to do a book in the ART & INSPIRATIONS series for C&T Publishing, I was thrilled to have this unique opportunity to reflect upon the people and past events that directed my career. My family and friends, through their encouragement, have given me confidence to explore new vistas. I began my journey as an artist with great trepidation. I was the one who always said, categorically, "I can't draw, therefore I can't paint or be an artist." This statement proved to all who would listen that I was in fact a nurse by college education without training in the arts. Little did I know that an artist can be defined in many ways.

MY FAMILY WAS COMPOSED OF MY FATHER, MY MOTHER, AN OLDER SISTER, and myself. Everyone in my family was very instrumental in starting the processes that I would later utilize in my art profession. My father, a very inventive man, was a jack-of-all-trades. There wasn't anything that he couldn't fix. Our family of four, the Bechis 4, (pronounced Beck-his) worked in our neighborhood bicycle and saw-sharpening shop. Besides dealing with the public, we all helped with the assembling of new bicycles, as well as repairs of bikes brought into the shop. Among the other family projects, one such included the preparation of our family Christmas greetings. My father and mother designed our annual Christmas card, and my sister and I helped cut and paste these lovely handmade creations. As I look back on the scrapbook of cards, I see both my mother's and father's talents in the design sketches, although at the time, I did not perceive my parents as "artists."

Now I realize that my father, Louis A. Bechis, had the remarkable talent of being able to market himself effectively. In particular, I recall an incident in the year of 1948. Dad purchased a 1937 Ford pickup truck, which he painted bright red. The shop's name, East Lake Cyclery, was prominently displayed on both of the doors. At Christmas time he would tie a huge, red cellophane bow onto the roof of the truck and drive around town advertising for all to see that the truck was the delivery wagon for Santa Claus. On Christmas Eve, after having assembled all the previously ordered new bicycles, our family set out to deliver each of these bicycles to their respective homes so they would be a surprise for the children. My mother would drive the pickup, and Dad would be in the passenger seat reading the specific delivery directions to each house. My sister, Marilou, and I would be sitting in the back of the truck holding onto the bicycles, lest they bang into each other and scratch the paint. At each house my father would park the truck, get out, and carry the bicycle to the house. The easiest deliveries were those where the garage door was open; Dad just left the bicycle in the garage and got back into the truck. The most difficult delivery was when he had to leave the bicycle on the front doorstep and ring the doorbell. Mother would start coasting down the street in the truck with the lights off while Dad would ring the bell, then run to catch up with the truck and jump in before anyone could see him. I can only imagine what joy we brought to those children.

**For Monique Eileen, (detail)**

When my mother, Mary Kalich Bechis, was a high school student she produced two works of art under the direction of her art teacher, Sister Veronica of the Sacred Heart. I inherited the two paintings, a pastel rendering of an English home and garden, and a small oil painting reproduction of a famous picture entitled *The End of the Trail*, and had them on display in our home for many years. I do not recall other paintings done by my mother except for the collaborative effort of a "paint by number" trio. When I was in grade school, our family received a painting kit that contained one large and two small white canvases. Each canvas featured a design printed in pale blue ink. The designs were irregularly shaped, and each shape had a number printed in it that corresponded to a specific paint color. The idea was to apply the paint carefully in the correct shape according to the number. I watched as my older sister, mother, and father transformed the canvases into colorful landscapes. The paintings hung over the couch in our living room for many years.

My mother was always very insistent that her girls be accomplished in sewing, knitting, and crocheting at an early age. At age nine, my summer project was to sew a gathered skirt under her direction. After three tries, she was satisfied that the skirt was made to her standards. From then on, my mother guided and encouraged me with each subsequent home-sewn project.

Until age eleven I shared a bedroom with my sister. When I wanted a room of my own, my parents agreed to let me transform the back porch into my own bedroom. I made six window curtains for that room, which helped keep out the draft and made the room cozy. I loved having my own room, even though it was less than perfect with its plain linoleum floor. I can still remember the feeling of stepping onto the small throw rug my mother gave me to protect my bare feet from the cold floor each morning. These simple beginning sewing projects soon led to sewing my own blouses and dresses.

Many years later, I elevated my skills in sewing to new heights. I learned to tailor my own clothes and even taught myself how to tailor a sport coat for my husband, Bob. Although my efforts were valiant, and he wore the jacket as needed, we soon found out that my knowledge of fitting a jacket to a man's body was nonexistent. I decided to leave men's tailoring to professionals and to concentrate on sewing for myself and our children.

While Bob was in the military, I enhanced my skills by challenging myself with new projects. A neighbor, whose husband also served in the military, became a springboard for artistic competitions. Our station was located at a remote outpost in Michigan, and sewing occupied a great part of our time. My husband was a flight surgeon and served his "call" nights on duty at the hospital, and my neighbor's husband, who was a navigator, served "on alert." My friend, Harlene Anthony, had been a professional artist, and she challenged me to become inventive in my sewing. If she embroidered her initials on the lining of her suit jacket, I would invent elaborate handmade buttons for mine. Eventually I taught her how to knit, and she encouraged me to try oil painting. This was a giant step for me, since up to that time the word artist translated into knowing how to draw, and I just knew I did not have any artistic talent. With her help (and much to my surprise), I painted a beautiful painting, which still hangs in our home. I will always remember her words to me: "You do so many routine chores during the course of a day. If you can do one creative thing for yourself that pleases you, it will make your life abundant."

Through the succeeding years I have discovered that abundance, and I am fortunate that I have learned to draw upon that which inspires me and to transform it into something tangible. I have learned that my art is my own personal language in the expression of color and shape. I do not question where this language comes from; I only understand that certain ideas may have served as resources. The mechanics of creating art seem to flow naturally, but when I look at a finished work, it is difficult to answer the question of how and why I made certain choices that make the art piece complete. My sense of creativity has developed through experimentation. Each idea leads to another, and with each successfully completed project, I have a need to try something new. This has become my creative challenge.

This book offers an overview of my use of color and imagery in weavings, wearables, and quilts. I hope that you enjoy reading the stories behind the work.

# DESIGN SOURCES:

where

have you

been,

and

what

did you

see?

SINCE THE EARLY 1970s, I HAVE BEEN INVITED TO TEACH MY TECHNIQUES to others in this country and around the world. It has been a great journey full of surprises. When I began this odyssey, it was from an instinctive need to be creative. Certainly I had no idea that my ability to sew would lead to such an interesting adventure. I have wonderful memories of important events and places or things that have served as inspiration.

As a child, I grew up in a small town in California near the Pacific Ocean, where my maternal grandmother, Rose Biele Kalich, was involved in the family business of growing produce in the fertile Pajaro Valley. Apples, lettuce, carrots, and other row crops—the mainstay of her farms in Watsonville—were marketed around the country. "Big Patch" was one of the brand names used to decorate the ends of produce boxes. I have recollections of going to that mysterious place called the packing shed, a long building on the edge of town where the produce was sorted, boxed, and shipped. Looking back, I realize this was also the first place where I recognized the beauty of similar forms and shapes arranged in an orderly fashion, each variety or type of produce in a box, with the colorful label announcing the family brand.

Along with memories of going to the packing shed, I noticed that calla lilies grew in profusion everywhere in Watsonville. They grew in my grandmother's backyard on West Lake Avenue, and they caught my eye each day as I walked to school. No one ever seemed to tend these plants; they just existed. Now, many years later, I use the image of the lily in many of my quilts as a remembrance of those early grammar school days.

My family never anticipated that I would attend a university. Since the age of five, my intention had always been to become a nurse. As I grew older, my goal was to attend a three-year nursing program where education was supplemented with hospital practice. My maternal grandfather, M. L. Kalich, passed away when I was two, and when I was five, my paternal grandfather, Enos Bechis, became gravely ill. Perhaps my decision to become a nurse came from a need to take care of my grandfather. When I was older, I took delight in accepting the responsibility of caring for him when my grandmother, Denise Mirassou Bechis, asked. During my high school years, I set up a program whereby I could volunteer as a junior aid in the local

hospital. After high school I had intentions of enrolling in St. Mary's School of Nursing in San Francisco. At that time, the three-year program combined education with service and hospital experience. My application was accepted with one addendum: my parents were to join me at a meeting with the Dean. At the meeting it was strongly suggested that I enter a degree nursing program at the university level to complete a one-and-a-half-year course of academics before entering the three-year school of nursing. The choice was not mine; my parents, who accepted this challenge for me, were wise enough to give me no alternatives.

A month after enrollment, our class attended a meeting where we were informed that a new four-year university School of Nursing program was under development, and we were to be the first attending students. What formally was a university with an all male student body was now to be a fully integrated male and female institution. We, the seventeen women, became the "pioneer" class. Each subsequent year a new class of nursing students was added, and eventually all schools and majors within the university included male and female students. Being the first female class lent itself to experiences too numerous to mention, but we all completed the course and passed the nursing boards, which allowed the school to become accredited.

Immediately after my graduation from nursing school, I married Robert S. Porcella, who had graduated from medical school at the same time. During Bob's internship, I worked as a full-time nurse until the birth of our first child, Stephen. Except for two years while Bob was in military service, I worked on a part-time basis over the next twenty years; my specialty was operating room nursing.

In 1962 my husband's military service ended. We returned to the central valley of California and bought a small home in Modesto. By this time we also had a two-year-old daughter, Suzanne (born in 1960), and shortly after moving, our son Gregory was born. Within the next year we had another son, Donald. With four children born during a four-and-a-half-year period, our new home proved to be too small. After several years, my husband and I decided to move to the country, just outside the city limits. We purchased an almond ranch, which would give us plenty of space to raise our family. As a child, I enjoyed visiting my paternal grandparents, who owned an almond ranch in Stanislaus County.

My grandfather was well known in the community. Beginning in 1927, he hosted an almond festival at his San Joaquin Valley ranch for eleven years. Often times a local dance group would perform. A 1928 *San Francisco Chronicle* newspaper article announced the annual event, stating that this was a good day's outing, and that all the roads were paved from the city to the small town of Oakdale.

The almond tree's gift to the world each spring is a profusion of fragrant blossoms. In Modesto, the trees bloom in mid-February, and for miles around you can see acres and acres of white trees, the rounded shapes of the canopy of branches bursting with flowers. While living among this natural splendor, I enjoyed photographing the beauty of the bloom. Perhaps this set the mood for my style of silk painting—translating soft pastel colors into painted quilts. (See *A World Beyond the Clouds*, page 120, and *Floating World*, page 118.)

Although I continued to sew the childrens' clothes and my own clothes, including suits and coats, after our two years of military service I made a decision. Rather than take the risk of making a garment from commercially produced fabric, only to see someone else wearing the same print, I would learn to make my own fabrics. When we returned to California from Michigan, I taught myself how to weave fabric. At the time, I didn't understand where this lofty confidence came from. Despite the fact that I could knit proficiently, I certainly knew nothing about the woven web. I borrowed a small twelve-inch-wide, two-harness loom and set out to make my cloth. Seeing a notice of a weavers' exhibition in the local paper, I sought them out and promptly asked how I could string my loom. I used pink and green cotton threads for the warp and many different textured yarns for the weft. With seven yards of the twelve-inch-wide woven cloth, I was able to make a skirt and vest. Thank goodness for the assistance and generosity of these wonderful women, because I soon became competent at the task, and for my first attempt won a ribbon at the regional competition.

Through the next few years, after exhausting the possibilities of a small loom, I advanced to a larger loom and began to design my own fabrics. I began to collect ethnic textiles, which served as my education in color and design for hand-woven cloth. I made many hand-woven outfits and even developed a new tech-

Many factors led to my interest in weaving. Throughout my career, a single event has often sparked a change in direction. This was true in my decision to learn how to weave. When my husband was in military service, we were transferred to Michigan; we arrived on December 20, 1960. The deep snows of the upper midwest were new to us native Californians, and learning to navigate icy roads was a challenge. At the base hospital, my husband had met another officer who lived with his wife next door to us. When I called my mother to tell her we had neighbors from the "wheat fields of the midwest" her comment was, "Oh, they are salt of the earth." I took that to mean that since Sally canned (hot-packed) her own tomatoes, she came from

traditions other than my own; nevertheless, we became friends.

The town adjacent to the base had only three stores: a grocery store, a hardware store, and a 5-and-10-cent general store. What you couldn't find in the hardware store was available in the general store, except for fabric and thread (other than black and white). Although I was firmly established in my upstairs sewing room, busy with all sorts of inventive projects, finding suitable fabric was near impossible. Mail order or packages sent from home were the best resources other than the eight-hour round-trip drive to Detroit. For my birthday in the late spring of the next year, my sister sent me a piece of fabric. It was mauve and lavender, a beautiful, muted swirled pattern, printed on

cotton voile. She even included matching thread because she knew I wouldn't have the exact color on hand. Excited by the possibilities I could envision, I ordered a Vogue pattern by mail. I had just enough fabric to make the sleeveless, bandeau neckline, wraparound dress. With pattern and fabric in hand, I set out to make a dress to wear to the June party at the Officer's Club. I learned to sew with the help of my mother, and we assumed if the pattern fit the model on the cover of the envelope, and our measurements were correct, the pattern would fit me. It seems strange now, but we never made a practice pattern to try on before cutting our special fabric. I didn't even consider that this new dress wouldn't fit right. After the customary stitching

nique for tapestry weaving which I called "nail loom weaving." In 1972, I was offered a commission from *Better Homes & Gardens* magazine to make a loom and weave a rug that was to be used for a photography spread in the August 1973 issue. I recall walking proudly with my mother down Market Street in San Francisco, carrying my 6' x 3' "new loom," and my mother carrying the rug, which we delivered to the West Coast editor. Later, the directions to make the frame and instructions on how to weave the rug appeared in the *Better Homes & Gardens* 1975 spring/summer *100's of Ideas Do-it-yourself* special issue.

**Colors of Nature**

In 1974, I designed a pin loom weaving technique that allowed me to make a two-sided collar. The warp was stretched over a board; the front was woven and shoulders shaped, and then the back was woven on one continuous warp. I used hand spun yarn and dyed it myself, inspired by the colors seen at the edge of Dry Creek in Modesto after a recent flood. It is decorated it with Pre-Columbian spinning whorls. Elyse Sommer featured this technique and the collar in her 1976 book *Wearable Crafts*.

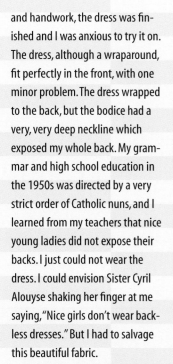

and handwork, the dress was finished and I was anxious to try it on. The dress, although a wraparound, fit perfectly in the front, with one minor problem. The dress wrapped to the back, but the bodice had a very, very deep neckline which exposed my whole back. My grammar and high school education in the 1950s was directed by a very strict order of Catholic nuns, and I learned from my teachers that nice young ladies did not expose their backs. I just could not wear the dress. I could envision Sister Cyril Alouyse shaking her finger at me saying, "Nice girls don't wear backless dresses." But I had to salvage this beautiful fabric.

Quickly I went to the general store to see what I could do. Maybe I could find a curtain or tablecloth I could do something with to make a cover-up. Finally I settled on a white nylon cardigan sweater and a bottle of purple Rit® dye. I would dye the sweater purple and wear it over the dress!

When the sweater came out of the washing machine it was not a beautiful purple but rather a pathetic shade of "pink mauve." It looked as if I had tried to dye a white sweater purple and it didn't work. The buttons screamed out as white shiny circles, surely announcing my failure to the world.

I re-examined the remaining fabric and thought that maybe if I pieced the scraps, I could trim the sweater with them. I cut off the buttons, as well as the opposite side of button holes, the hem, and the cuffs. Confidently I pieced together tiny scraps of fabric and stitched them as binding over the cut edges. And it worked! Not a perfect color match, but it did give me an ensemble. I proudly wore the dress and matching sweater, comfortable in the knowledge that my back did not show. At the June party, I accepted compliments about my matching outfit, and needless to say, I never removed the sweater.

A few weeks later, my neighbor announced that her mother and grandmother were driving from their home to visit, and should I be looking out my sewing room window when a strange car pulled up, I would recognize them as her kinfolk. I should say that at this time in my life (my early twenties) a mother and grandmother were certainly old folks to me.

When the car arrived, I noted from my window that the driver got out of the car to help the "older woman" out of the passenger side . . . mother and grandmother had arrived. Oh no! Grandmother had on a dress made from the same beautiful fabric as my recently completed ensemble! I rushed outside to say hello and to admire the older woman's dress. "Oh, this dress," she said, "we only have one store in my hometown and you can get just about anything there—hardware, groceries, or dry goods in the back. I bought this off the rack."

This single event inspired my motivation to learn how to create my own fabric. In the future, when wearing my ensembles, I would never again encounter anyone else wearing the same fabric.

Texture is a fundamental aspect of weaving. The art is in selecting the combination of different types of yarn that give the woven cloth its texture. A weaver likes to feel the hand of the fabric and see the drape. Pattern is another integral part of the weaving process, with the range extending from a simple balanced warp/weft to complex multi-harness combinations. I enjoyed weaving for about eighteen years, and although I retired as a weaver in 1980, I still am attracted to textural and patterned surfaces. It was because of my experience as a weaver that I began the odyssey of teacher, artist, and author. Beginning in 1971, I traveled throughout California demonstrating my weaving techniques, and eventually teaching collaged clothing.

Something seen—a brief interlude in a store, a trip to a museum—always sparked an idea for new ways to use color. Color was my starting point. As a weaver, I enjoyed working in bright colors; stripes and plaids were my specialty. The items featured on page 12 are all handwovens using red as the dominant color theme. My love of texture is found in these examples. Mohair, a type of yarn which is lightweight but very warm, was my favorite thread. It has always been popular to use in throws or stoles, and I knew I could make a stole in a relatively short period of time, since mohair requires an open weave rather than a densely packed weave.

Some time later when I attempted a double weave web (a two-sided fabric with a different pattern or color on each side), I selected a wool knitting yarn brought back from England by my mother. I valiantly wove the stole, but when it was removed from the loom, I noticed the selvage (where the color changed from the back to the front) of the stole was very uneven. I solved this problem by first crocheting an edging and then adding handmade tassels to all four sides of the stole.

For the vest made in 1975, I warped the loom with different colored cotton threads and used a red weft thread to make the fabric. I used the same colored threads to make small dolls using three inch-wide bands of woven cotton striped fabric. (See *Rainbow Woven Dolls*, page 59.)

After finishing a weaving project there were always bits and pieces of different colored threads left over. I always tried to recycle these leftover threads using a continuous buttonhole stitch, called knotless netting. To make the stitch with wool yarns, I used a large-eyed blunt needle. I was able to make a pair of gloves using this stitch; my left hand served as the form.

The joy of traveling is experiencing the sights and sounds of new vistas. When I see something interesting, I like to capture it on film to serve as a future resource. The city of San Diego is itself a colorful destination where the flowers are a feast for the eyes. Bougainvillea is a vigorous climbing vine, which colors the landscape of this Southern California city. While visiting Carol Martin at her home there, I could not resist taking a photo of such a perfect contrast of color and texture. During the 1960s and 1970s, my dream as a weaver was to visit Cranbrook Academy of Art in Michigan. When, in 1981, I had an exhibition of wearable art in a gallery in Birmingham, Michigan, I visited the campus and photographed a red bush, which serves as a vivid memory of my visit.

After years of studying the ethnic costumes and textiles in my collection, which served as inspiration for my weavings, I was ready to explore the artful tradition of the Japanese kimono. Through the centuries, the pattern for the kimono style garment has not changed, but every type of surface design has been executed. Pieced fabrics, woven fabrics, hand-dyed fabrics, and embroidery are all found in antique kimonos. In 1979, I became interested in exploring kimono patterns, and I made a patchwork haori coat, the outer garment worn over the kimono. From 1980 to 1986, "Kimono as Quilt" became a theme of my artwork, and in early 1986, I was finally able to visit Kyoto, Japan. Although I thought I was prepared for what I might see, Japan proved to be a visual feast. Texture and color can be found everywhere—from the stalls of flea market vendors to the sacred shrines. Wonderfully shaped trees, artfully planted for color in landscape, are images that will stay with me forever.

Natural scenic beauty—how a tree gracefully etches the blue sky, a beautiful sunset, flowers in all forms—feeds my soul. They may not transfer directly into my art, but are certainly a part of my design source. Bob and I are fortunate to live very close to Yosemite National Park. Even though I was born in California, it wasn't until my first son was born that I visited the grandeur of this place. As our children grew older, we spent many summer vacations backpacking on the eastern slopes of the park.

# shadows

## of

# forgotten

## ancestors

DURING MY DAYS OF COLLECTING TEXTILES, MY ATTRACTION WAS TO THE bright, colorful hand-woven fabrics of native peoples. These were very easy to purchase in the 1960s, since this was the time of President Kennedy's Peace Corps, the youth of America educating and helping to modernize third-world cultures. These young Americans were traveling and exploring exotic places, and would often buy the local goods. They soon discovered that money could be made by selling these items upon returning to the States. Weavers and textile enthusiasts were anxious to invest in the treasures of other civilizations, many not seen before in America. It was one thing to study books or view the exotic on the pages of *National Geographic*, but quite another to experience the fabrics firsthand. Molas from the San Blas Islands were plentiful, as were fabrics woven in Guatemala and Mexico. Also abundant were ikat fabrics from Burma, printed textiles from Indonesia, and embroideries from Bedouin tribes. My favorite treasures were pieced and embroidered textiles from Uzbekistan and Afghanistan. A prized piece from my collection is an embroidered bag from Uzbekistan.

The annual conference of hand weavers in Northern California featured guild exhibits of the best of that year's hand-woven textiles, as well as a merchants' mall. The mall was the place to buy new weaving threads and equipment. Gradually vendors came with diverse fabrics collected during their nomadic trips. This was the "Age of Aquarius," or so we were told by the "hippie generation." It was time to wear this "ethnic" stuff which paired very nicely with denim jeans or indigo-dyed skirts from Guatemala.

As a collector, I selected flat textiles so I could examine the woven structure. I knew these beautiful fabrics, created from a living tradition, could teach me something if I looked closely enough. Eventually, I began to purchase handmade costumes for my collection. My earliest book, *Five Ethnic Patterns* (1977), featured contemporary garment patterns based on clothing from my collection. My interest was in the width of the woven cloth and how that could be divided into the pieces for the pattern. I was determined to find ways to use my hand-woven fabric to its best advantage without cutting too deeply into the cloth.

A very important resource for me during these days were books featuring folk costumes. *Cut My Côte*, from the Royal Ontario Museum in Toronto, helped me identify garment construction. *Costume Patterns and Designs*, by Max Tilke, was and still is one of my favorite resources.

After the first few years of weaving my own wool and silk fabrics from which I made elaborate outfits, I reached a dilemma. These heirlooms were beginning to impact on my closet space, and certainly I could not rid myself of anything I had made. In fact, someday my family would inherit them, and they too would have to find storage space. The solution seemed to be to switch my focus to weaving tapestries and smaller accessories. As for my wearable art, I decided to incorporate cotton textiles woven by others. (Beginning in 1971, when I demonstrated weaving and hand spinning to local community groups and schoolchildren, I found that it was more comfortable to wear a colorful pieced dress rather than a heavier hand-woven garment.)

In 1972, I had my first gallery exhibition of woven items and wearable art. The garments, which were made from a mixture of ethnic textiles, were the hit of the show. I sold most of the garments and very few of the weavings. Each floor-length dress included many types of fabrics. I would combine mirror cloth from

Kutch, Guatemalan hand-woven cottons, woven decorative trims from Germany, and ikat from Bhutan. The dresses were made using my concept of collage; decorative braids or trims were cut, layered, and stitched over other fabrics to join the fragments together. In some cases, the lower edge of a sleeve might have ten different trims or fabrics included in a nine-inch cuff.

Reflecting on my childhood, I remember seeing textile designs from other cultures. During the late 1940s, my grandmother traveled and brought back treasures from exotic places. She bought an embroidered blouse for me in Trieste, which I loved and wore in my youth and enjoyed wearing again during my period as a textile collector. The blouse looked quite chic with a pair of denim jeans. In 1946, my father worked as a seed salesman in Mexico, and he would always bring gifts home for the family. My mother made matching outfits for herself and my sister and me out of fabric he brought back. In my own textile collection, there are many pieces that spark a memory for me. I know which purchases had great impact on my future work, such as a magenta, silk-embroidered nomad dress from Afghanistan, a pieced tunic from Nuristan, a mirror shirt from India, and handwoven huipils from Oaxaca and Guatemala.

**Family photo, 1947**

During the 1970s, several shops in the San Francisco Bay Area sold folk textiles and costumes. Thousand Cranes and Shadows of Forgotten Ancestors were two shops that specialized in selling the exotic. Many years ago when prices were reasonable, I purchased molas to use in my early garments. Eventually I decided to keep a few as a collection. The mola color combinations served as inspiration for my garments. In the photo on the right, tiny mola pieces, decorative ribbons, and Guatemalan fabrics were used to decorate a vest and woman's top. Both patterns are featured in *Pieced Clothing* (1980), my book on clothing patterns. The vest has small areas where the stripe woven fabric has been pieced to make blocks.

When I began patchwork, I had to learn how to buy "quilter's fabric." I was not interested in purchasing the tiny calico prints I saw used in old quilts. My cupboards were full of exotic fabrics from all over the world. I thought that if I began with solid-colored fabrics, I could make the color work for me by using simple pieced patterns. Hand appliqué was a technique I had learned as a child, but quilt block piecing was a different story.

The first thing I did was invest in a collection of solid-colored fabrics. I selected 150 colors from a packet of mail-order quilter's cotton samples, and ordered one yard of each. (This shop was called Cabin Fever Calicos and the proprietor was Elly Sienkiewicz.) I thought that all these colors would provide a palette from which to make my selections. If I needed more color for a project, I could supplement the first yard. Next, I would buy a print that I liked and then pull solid colors from my collection to enhance the print. Most often I bought large-scale prints because of my dislike of the small-scale calicos.

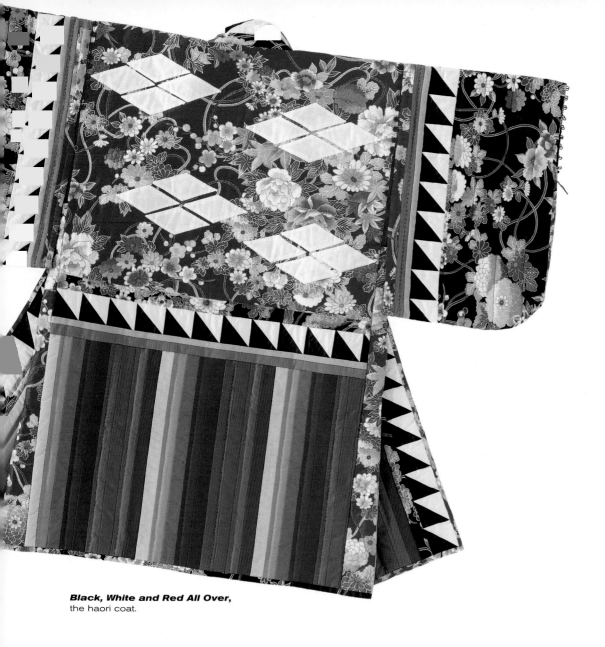

**Black, White and Red All Over,**
the haori coat.

*Five Ethnic Patterns* and *Plus Five* (the books I printed in 1977 and 1978) featured sample garments in my collage style, made from ethnic textiles. The reason for printing my own books was simply a matter of convenience. When I taught collage clothing classes, I had more than five pages of pattern directions to hand out. Often I would get a phone call from a student who had misplaced one of the pages. Printing the patterns in a book was the answer.

The concept of printing my own books seemed logical at the time. I knew nothing about the process, but I had a wonderful printer who helped me understand the necessary steps. I set up the pages and indicated where the type should be placed in relation to the drawing. The printer retyped my instructions, and I pasted them in place on the printer's boards.

In 1980, when I began to make the sample garments for *Pieced Clothing*, I put my collection of solid-colored fabrics to good use. This new book featured patchwork designs expanding on my style of garment construction, which was based on folk costume patterns. The fourteen patterns in the book were made using cotton fabrics in either solid color or large prints. A patchwork Japanese haori coat was featured on the cover of the book.

I also published this book myself, had it printed on a web press (the minimum press run was 10,000 copies), and set about to sell the inventory. Again, I do not know where the confidence came from that my uneducated marketing strategy would work, but somehow, I sold out the inventory in less than a year, and the book was reprinted many times. *Pieced Clothing Variations* was printed in 1981 and featured a single vest pattern with ten variations on how to make it into jackets or coats.

For many years I had success teaching my style of collage garment construction from *Five Ethnic Patterns* and *Plus Five* (a second book printed in 1978), to guilds of fiber artists, stitchers, weavers, and quilters. My first attempt at a pieced quilted garment came when I was invited to include a quilt in the teachers' exhibit at the 1979 West Coast Quilter's conference. The only quilts I had made up to that point were, thankfully, never seen by the public, but rather, were private gifts to friends. I really did not know much about the art of patchwork.

Nine Patch seemed like a good place to begin. How difficult could it be? Just sew nine squares of fabric together. I did not know the patches should be sewn in a pattern, with perhaps all the corners and the center cut from one fabric. I decided I would make a pieced haori coat (quilts were not my forte), because wearable art was what I was teaching. I selected a beige fabric for the center panel of the coat and appliquéd a crane on the front and back. I made enough Nine Patch blocks to begin designing the pieced sleeves. When it came time to select a batting, again without experience, I selected a very stiff batting. *Two Cranes Coat* was wonderful, except for a minor problem only recognized after it was finished: it was not wearable! When the coat was on, the batting was so stiff you had to extend your arms out to the sides because the fabric would not bend and conform to the body. No one at the exhibition ever noticed, since the coat was hung on a rod that ran through the center panel and sleeves. I had made a T-shaped quilt!

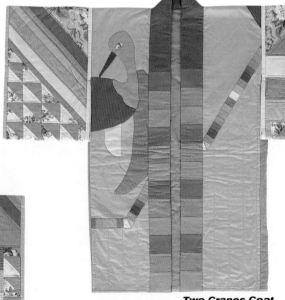

**Two Cranes Coat**
(back and front views)

**①**

**③**

1. **Harlequin Jacket**

2. **Over the Rainbow**

3. **Coral Coat**

4. **Tekke**

**1**

**2**

1. *Red Jacket*
2. *Short Sleeve Jacket*
3. *China Doll*

The most fun for me in making wearables was to expand on my basic patterns. Perhaps because I had designed the patterns from a folk costume tradition, I liked the idea of making a curved line, drawn upon the flat pattern shape, which would alter the shape. Using my first vest pattern, which appeared in *Five Ethnic Patterns*, I expanded it into ten patterns in *Pieced Clothing Variations*. In 1982 I designed a full-size jacket pattern by adding fitted sleeves to the basic vest. *Six Color World* (1997) features instructions for my jacket pattern. Bringing the full sleeve pattern from my 1972 wearable art dresses onto the vest and adding a gathered peplum is another idea for expanding on the basic pattern. See *Harlequin Jacket* and *Coral Coat*, page 30. The *Short Sleeve Jacket* and *Over the Rainbow* are variations of other patterns.

The white chevron patchwork strips in *Tekke*, page 31 (which was featured on the cover of *Pieced Clothing Variations*), were pieced by hand in a method I developed to replicate the pieced pattern found in an Afghanistan textile in my collection. Three strips of chevron piecing were added to other bits and pieces of patchwork.

When I began to make patchwork units to use in garments, I would often have leftover pieces. I would store them in a box for future use, just as I had saved leftover weaving threads. I named these garments "Chop Suey" style, meaning bits and pieces of leftovers tossed together to make a whole. *China Doll*, a "Chop Suey" style garment, has two surfaces; the outside is pieced and the inside features a drawing of metallic pen on black fabric.

**Papa Natalé nel Giardino**

*Memories*

Throughout my career I have been asked to submit garments for the Fairfield Processing Corporation Fashion Show, which showcases annually at Quilt Market and Quilt Festival in Houston, Texas. In the early years, the show was co-sponsored by Concord Fabrics. At that time, the selected fabrics were sent to the artists to make their garments. The fabrics sent to me were all tiny calico prints, which I could not imagine trying to use. These fabrics looked just like the small calico quilt prints I was trying to avoid when I began making patchwork. I supplemented these with one slightly larger print of a Santa Claus. I cut the prints into as many small pieces as I could. To satisfy my need for brighter colors and a bolder look, I went to a local fabric store and looked at all the selvages until I found a fabric with "Concord" printed on the edge. At last, I found a bold print I was happy to use. I used my Tibetan coat pattern from *Pieced Clothing*, with the tiny calico prints and Santa Claus on one side and the bold look on the other with black and white pieced half square triangles, which is based on the patchwork found in an antique Afghanistan textile. The finished coat is called *Papa Natalé nel Giardino* (Santa Claus in the Garden). Fairfield recently celebrated twenty years of sponsorship of the fashion show. Each one of the garments I made for the show reflects my interest in fabric or pattern. I thought I would share with you some of my favorite pieces. *Memories* coat,

From left:

*Kaleidoscopically
Yours*

*Carnival*

*How Old Are You
Now?*

*Walking the Streets
of Tomorrow*

made in 1981, uses one large, tropical floral print with the Concord-designed micro dot fabric in seven colors. For *Kaleidoscopically Yours*, the fitted pattern is from the 1982 Jacket Pattern; it combines white fabrics and features a pieced front and back panel overlay, which is bound with pieced binding. The skirt is an original pattern, which wraps around and can be worn either white- or colorful patchwork-side out.

For *Carnival*, made in 1987, I wanted the outfit to have an overall appearance of purple when the model first walked out onto the runway. Then the jacket could be removed to show the colorful tunic pieced with Log Cabin blocks and strip piecing. The purple silk skirt is lined with chartreuse and orange netting to give fullness at the hem.

On the occasion of the tenth anniversary of the Fairfield Fashion Show in 1988, I made a garment titled *How Old Are You Now?*, featuring a printed panel from a Happy Birthday fabric, which explains the title. Parts of the jacket have the printed birthday fabric, which is surrounded with colorful checkerboard piecing. The pedal pusher pants remind us of that popular, but older, fashion fad.

In 1990 I made *Walking the Streets of Tomorrow*, which refers to recycling —I made the vest using leftover scraps of fabric. The blouse is recycled from an outfit made in 1980. By changing the patchwork on the lower sleeves, I could recycle the blouse to be worn ten years later.

Wearables have been an important part of my career, both with the development of my garment patterns and in creating colorful collaged and patchwork clothing. I also made garments with the intention they would never be worn. These I call "Kimono as Quilt."

## 3

TWO EVENTS SERVED AS THE CATALYST FOR THE WORK WHICH I CALL "Kimono as Quilt." First, my interest in surface design and fabrics used in the Japanese kimono led me to a book which included an illustration of a sixteenth-century Dofuku (a specific style of kimono). The photograph suggested the antique kimono was made from patchwork. Second, a trip to The Asian Art Museum in San Francisco to see an exhibition of "Traditional Japanese Folk Art" had great impact on me when I noticed the title of one kimono, *Bedding of Kimono Form.* This kimono, or sleeping quilt, larger than normal body size, was filled with a futon (a thick padding), so it could be laid over the body for warmth.

During the two-hour drive home from the museum, I contemplated the concept of making a quilt, but in the shape of a kimono. By now I had a limited knowledge of patchwork; I had made a haori, the Japanese coat worn over a kimono. I had collected kimonos for their beauty of surface color and design, and I had a very old kimono pattern book with instructions in Japanese. What finally worked for me was to take one of my collected kimonos, lay it on my studio floor, measure it, and draft a pattern. From my years of working with folk costumes, I was able to calculate the pieces necessary to make the pattern. With my interest in patchwork, I decided to make the kimono using contemporary fabrics rather than traditional fourteen-inch-wide Japanese fabrics. I began piecing flat rectangular shapes, two 12" x 36" and two 24" x 60". If the experiment failed, the rectangles could be sewn together to make a regular quilt.

Because of my interest in wearable art, I saw the kimono as an opportunity to create a three-dimensional object—the kimono-clad body-in-motion—making a moving sculpture. From this perspective, I decided to design each panel so that it stood by itself—back, sleeves, and front. All the pieces had to integrate as a whole, with color and patchwork giving it unity.

Another factor for investing so much energy in my kimono as quilt concept was that when not worn, the Japanese kimono traditionally was shown on a beautiful kimono stand. My fantasy was that perhaps I could tap into this ancient culture, one that preserved its wearable costume and displayed it as art. Also the shape of the hanging kimono offered many possibilities. It could be shown as a simple T-shape, which appealed to me from my study of folk costume. Or, the fronts could be opened and secured to either the wall or the kimono stand to make interesting triangular patterns within the rectangular shape. I thought I was in heaven. Finally I could begin.

My first attempt was to combine strip piecing with checkerboard blocks. I used a jumble of colors, but fortunately they all seemed to make a cohesive whole. I titled the piece *Bedding In Kimono Form* and included it in the showing of my quilts and wearables in early 1981. It was sold in 1984. The second kimono in the series illustrates my emphasis on analogous color featuring individual design motifs—Log Cabin blocks, Pinwheel blocks, and strip piecing—on each pattern piece. *Red Kimono* was shown in 1982 in New York at the American Craft Museum exhibition entitled, "Pattern, The Decorated Surface."

In subsequent kimonos, I experimented with patterns of color, each piece giving me a better understanding of patchwork and art. With the third kimono, I decided to make the interior (or lining) for the piece as interesting as the exterior design; not so elaborate as to interfere with the brilliance of the patchwork, but a design that would relate to the title or concept.

**Red Kimono, 60" x 48"**

1. *Hot Kimono,* 60" x 48"

2. *Cool Kimono,* 60" x 48"

After teaching at a quilting conference in Colorado in 1982, I came home and translated the energy I felt at the conference into a kimono. While working on the patchwork, I was struck with the emotion that I had just created a wonderful robe. I had read the science fiction books written by Anne McCaffrey celebrating the adventures of the Dragonriders of Pern. I could imagine the heroine of a McCaffrey book donning this robe after riding the dragons to save the planet from the dreaded "Threadfall." My kimono became *Robe For A Dragonrider*. It features cotton patchwork, with the color flow of pastels cascading from the collar to the hem of bright colors.

When it came time to prepare the lining for this piece, my wonderful artist friend, Steve Kalar, stopped by my studio and offered to paint a dragon for the lining. I hung over his shoulder, watching each brush stroke, offering unwarranted suggestions so that the painting would be perfect for installation inside my kimono.

Opposite: ***Robe For A Dragonrider*, 60" x 48"**

Below: ***When All The Colors Come Dancing*, 72" x 48"**

For *Hot Kimono* (page 39), I chose colors which were warm in feeling: yellows at the top and reds and purples at the hem. Nine-Patch blocks anchor the design. I stamped the silk lining with rectangle and square sponges, using textile paint to match the colors and pattern of the exterior patchwork. *Cool Kimono* (page 39) is a color mate to *Hot Kimono*. Fabrics were chosen to reflect a cool palette, and the color purple ties these two pieces together. Half-square triangles and strip piecing are set on the diagonal; the colors flow from the shoulder to the hem.

As each kimono became more elaborate, I decided that they should not be worn, but would be displayed on the wall as art. One way to guarantee that the kimonos would not be worn was to make them larger than life-size. I began by adding a few inches to the lengths. Then the batting became thicker to make them difficult to drape and tie with an obi. Finally I threw caution to the wind and made a kimono that no one could wear.

*When All The Colors Come Dancing* was such a kimono. The length is six feet long from neck to hem. The patchwork in this kimono began as an exercise in color, putting together thirty-six patch checkerboard blocks which, when sewn together, made one very large Nine Patch. After making three of these, boredom set in, and I decided to throw this formula out the window. The remainder of patchwork, just red and black, frames the colorful checkerboard blocks. Asymmetry won in the end. *When All The Colors Come Dancing* is in the collection of the Los Angeles County Museum of Art, Los Angeles, California.

Pasha On The 10:04 has a simple pieced exterior using just black, white, and red with small accents of rainbow colors. It also features a print fabric for the lining. One of the black and white figures was hand colored. *Midnight Celebration* uses half-square triangle piecing with strips of jewel tones and black fabric.

In 1986, my exceptionally large kimono was included in *The Art Quilt* exhibition curated by Michael Kile and Penny McMorris. The curators suggested that I make a kimono as large as eighteen feet, since the ceiling height of the first exhibition space would allow for that size. The finished kimono was a more manageable size, eleven feet tall by seven feet wide. It was made with six layers. First I made a kimono using silk fabric, a futon-type batting, and a pieced lining. This would be suspended on a three-inch diameter painted rod. Over this, twenty-two feet of patchwork would be placed which, when folded at the top and tied on the sides, made a pieced kimono cover. *Snow On Mt. Fuji* was the last kimono I made in patchwork style. It was featured as the entry piece (the first piece you see when you enter an exhibit) when it was installed at the opening venue at Barnsdall Park, Los Angeles, California. It is now a part of the collection of the American Craft

1.  Left: ***Pasha On The 10:04, 63" x 48"***
    Right: Interior view showing lining.

2.  ***Snow On Mt. Fuji, 11' x 7', 1985***

3.  ***Midnight Celebration, 60" x 48"***

Many of my kimonos were created using bright, solid-colored cotton fabrics, and subsequent kimonos had more elaborate decoration on the lining. This follows the ancient tradition in Japan of having an interesting fabric on the lining which was known only to the wearer. My favorite Japanese book is *The Tale of Genji*, written by Murasaki Shikibu in the tenth century. Many artists have been inspired by the work of Lady Murasaki, and through the centuries, Japanese artisans have honored her memory. In 1993, The Los Angeles County Museum of Art hosted the exhibition *When Art Became Fashion, Kosode in Edo-Period Japan*. In the catalog which accompanied the exhibition, it is noted that Miyazaki Yuzen, an artist-monk in the late 1600s, introduced literary images in textile design by painting pictures on silk kimonos for wealthy patrons using subject matter from *The Tale of Genji*.

I too was inspired to make a painted-silk kimono after reading passages in *The Tale of Genji*, which describe the colorful kimonos given by Genji as gifts to women known to him. I had made patchwork haori coats, the outer garment worn over the kimono, and patchwork kimono, all of them including bright colors. Making a kimono in patchwork or silk involves more time and effort; kimonos are long and wrap across the front. Haori, by comparison, is a relatively easy garment to make; it is shorter and worn with the front open. The length of the kimono sleeves changed throughout Japanese history, some sleeves were quite long and some were shorter. The sleeve length of the haori is dictated by the length of the kimono sleeve worn underneath. When making my kimono, the sleeve length was determined by both the surface design and the overall size; a bigger kimono needed longer sleeves.

Museum; New York, New York. Through the following years I made other kimonos using hand-painted silk. *Love Lingers Where The Water Flows*, on page 120, is one of these kimonos.

Firebird is the second of two kimonos I made with a dimensional surface. I was inspired to try this technique after I purchased an antique Victorian silk throw. The surface of the throw was covered with randomly cut pieces of thousands of silk scraps. The silk pieces were small triangular snips of plaid, plain, and textured silks. Each snip was hand stitched by catching just the point of each piece to a background fabric, overlapping rows of the silk to make a block. The blocks were covered with the silk and then edged with snips of black silk velvet. This extraordinary silk throw currently is in the quilt collection at the Los Angeles County Museum of Art, a gift from my husband and me, but it first served as inspiration to me for *Diamonds on Ice* (see page 123) and *Firebird*.

I found that randomly cut, new pieces of silk did not have the charm which I found in the antique Victorian throw. A contemporary piece had to have a new look. I compromised by cutting two-inch-wide bias strips of white silk pongee. I then cut each strip into two-inch diamonds. My next step was to cut kimono pattern pieces out of white muslin. I drew horizontal pencil lines, two inches apart, across each pattern piece. Twenty-four yards of silk pongee cut into two-inch diamond shapes were needed to decorate the kimono. I stitched overlapping rows of silk diamonds onto the muslin following the drawn lines, catching just the top edge of the diamond in the seam.

**Firebird, 72" x 48", 1984**

After covering the back, two fronts, and sleeves with diamond "petals," I pinned the pieces to my design wall and sprayed them with fabric paint in a distinctive color pattern: yellow in the center, then lavender and turquoise. After the paint was dry, I carefully sewed the kimono, keeping the diamond shapes out of the seams. I painted the lining pieces, added the batting, and used rhinestones to secure these layers together. I joined the layers at the neck edge in the collar seam and in the hem seam.

I honor the memory of Lady Murasaki with my pastel-colored silk kimono. The feathered kimono endeavors were a challenge to make and very dramatic when finished, but I do not envision the need to make another in this textured style.

WORKING WITH COLOR IS EXCITING FOR ME; IT IS WHERE I AM MOST comfortable. I learned color interaction from examining the process of weaving textiles, and this still serves as an unconscious reference point. I choose one color that I like and pull in other colors to create harmony. This process takes some time; I have to buy very specific colors or paint the fabric myself if needed. I believe years of practice have helped my confidence regarding color.

Although traditional quilting patterns serve as inspiration, I have never made a traditional quilt. This is probably because I grow tired of the precision necessary to repeat the same block many times. My expertise in quilt blocks is limited, and most of my work encompasses only a few traditional concepts. When I first began to make quilts, I used strips of fabric, accenting them with pieced triangles. I could play with strips of color and experiment with their relationship to each other.

I saw a Gene Davis painting in a museum, and I liked the fact that he limited himself to painting vertical stripes. To have painted the same stripes in a horizontal format would have reduced the energy I felt in viewing the vertical movement. The circa 1875 *Joseph's Coat* quilt featured in *New Discoveries In American Quilts* by Robert Bishop also intrigued me; I wanted to try to make a striped quilt.

*Takoage* was my first art quilt. Without a plan, I began sewing together pieces of fabrics cut 1½" or 2" wide in different lengths. I sewed these into strips 82" long. I kept sewing until I had enough long strips to make a 72" wide quilt top. I laid the long sewn strips on the floor of my studio and looked at the color play. I found that taking a Polaroid® picture helped me to see what these strips would look like when sewn together. A reducing glass was also a helpful tool. I would move around the vertical strips to different spots on the floor, or even open a seam to add another color. Once the composition seemed pleasing, I would sew the vertical rows together.

Sometimes for color accent, I added a folded Prairie Point into the vertical seam. I liked the folded texture which related to the pieced triangle blocks. When stitching this piece together along the vertical seams, I found that I had to sew two vertical long strips to make a pair and then sew two pairs together. I alternated the stitching lines from top to bottom and bottom to top when stitching the pairs together to prevent distorting the quilt top. I wanted to guarantee the same width at both the top and bottom edges. When I finished, I added batting and backing, but I couldn't decide what to do for the quilting stitch. The backing fabric was a heavy drapery fabric printed with Japanese kites. I turned the quilt to the lining side and quilted along the kite strings. You can see remnants of this fabric in *Over The Rainbow* on page 31. I did not know that you were not supposed to quilt from the back side! I entertained the philosophy that I was making an art quilt (even though no such term existed at that point), so therefore my quilting stitches were also art. Each stitch was a different length, and I wanted them to be as far apart as possible. Both the quilting stitches and the vertical stripes set this quilt apart from traditional style.

In 1994, this quilt was purchased through the Smithsonian Collection acquisition program for The Renwick Gallery of the Museum of American Art, Smithsonian Institution, Washington, D.C.

In January 1981, I had an exhibition of wearables and quilts at Patience Corners quilt shop in Berkeley, California, where my quilt *Takoage* was shown for

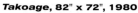
**Takoage, 82" x 72", 1980**

the first time. I wanted a snappy title for the show, and after much deliberation I settled on *Color/Cloth*. Knowing this would not be considered a traditional quilt show, I felt that color and cloth described what it was. My idea was to silk-screen a small block with that title and fix the fabric onto the invitations. I invited a printmaker to make the design for me and screen the design in two sizes, small and large. I used some of the blocks in quilts and garments created for the show. The large blocks made a banner, which hung in the window of the shop. Later I made a quilt out of the banner and gave it to the printmaker.

I began my patchwork experience with Nine Patch blocks, but the first attempt, shown in *Two Cranes Coat* (see page 29), was less than perfect. The Nine Patch concept was the focus for designing *Masquerade* (see page 50). The title alone should give away

the secret of the major design flaw. After making *Takoage* in the vertical strip format, I was ready to try a different set. The next attempt was to make nine equal-sized vertical strip-pieced blocks and sew them together. Was I surprised when I finished the stitching to see that the nine blocks were lost in the indistinguishable vertical

*Color/Cloth* banner,
60" x 60", 1980

seams, and only the horizontal seams were noticeable. Only the maker knows where the blocks are hiding. This quilt was included in *Influences,* an invitational exhibit held at the Spencer Museum of Art in 1982. Barbara Brackman and Chris Wolf Edmonds curated the show, which featured contemporary quilts hung along with the antique quilts that inspired the individual designs.

Yellow is a color that I had used sparingly in my early work. It seemed to be a difficult color to emphasize in the wearable art that was a large part of those early years. Yellow was always a component of my rainbow spectrum, but never the dominant color. One day I decided to make a yellow quilt to learn more about the color. I was working very hard on this challenge when a phone call interrupted my work. My exhausted and feeble "hello" indicated to the caller that I was indeed tired or maybe ill. No, just working on a yellow quilt! The break in concentration served its purpose, for when I returned to the design, it occurred to me that yellow needed to be alongside its complement color, purple, and why not try every color of the rainbow? *Homage To A Rainbowmaker* was the result. It features diagonal piecing interrupting the four vertical panels. Strip piecing using different fabric widths and folded Prairie Points were the basic structural elements used to design this piece.

*Masquerade, 64" x 64",*
**1982,** private collection

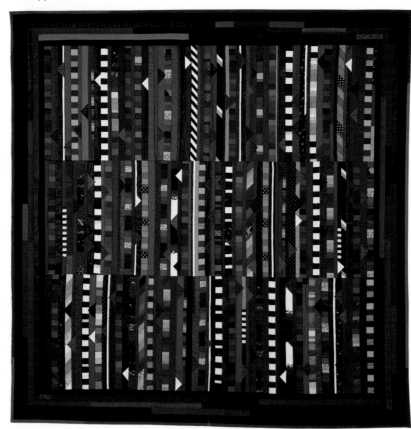

***Homage To A Rainbowmaker,***
**65" x 65", 1983,** collection of
Pat and Martha Connell

In 1984 I made *Ginza*, another quilt in the style of *Takoage*; that is, strips and pieced triangles sewn together in vertical rows. I appliquéd gold metallic fabric shapes over the patchwork. I was inspired by a picture of the Ginza region in Japan, which I saw in a book at my hostess' home during a 1970s teaching trip. In 1984, Patty Chase from Massachusetts was invited to curate The Contemporary Quilt exhibition of American art quilts to tour cities in Japan. *Ginza* was included in that exhibition. Upon her return from the show, Patty gave me the exhibition poster, which used my quilt to advertise the event.

Two other quilts made around the same time were strip pieced using wider vertical elements of patchwork. *Carro* includes Nine Patch blocks and a center rectangle of folded Prairie Points. *Polka Dot Fantasy* was a design exercise in limiting my palette to red, yellow, and blue, plus black and white. I added one strip of green fabric.

**Ginza, 67" x 67", 1984,**
collection of Nihon Vogue,
Tokyo, Japan

I learned how to make the folded Prairie Point while I was teaching in Redmond, Washington, in the late 1970s. Betty Ferguson introduced me to the Folded Star (Prairie Points overlapped in a circle which make a unique star pattern). The star itself did not appeal to me, but the concept of folding a square into a triangle shape was very intriguing. I came home and immediately put the single folded triangle to use in my work. I sewed it into the patchwork seams of a vest, which appeared in *Pieced Clothing* in 1980, and then added it to the vertical seams of *Takoage*.

Nancy Halpern sent me a photograph of a 1930s quilt that hung in an east coast quilt show. The whole surface was made using the folded Prairie Points. Of course this made the quilt very heavy, but the idea was still exciting. I decided to try using lots of Prairie Points, but to confine the folded triangles to the central medallion of a quilt.

Actually folding the Prairie Points gets pretty boring after the first few, and I tried to talk anyone coming into my studio into pressing them for me. For my quilt, I chose a woven cotton with an irregular stripe pattern. As a weaver, I loved to weave striped fabric, and the purchased fabric was a good color combination— red and pink. By cutting different portions of the stripe, I could vary the look of the folded Prairie Points. I added Nine Patch blocks and strip piecing as borders around the central panel. The result is *Carro*.

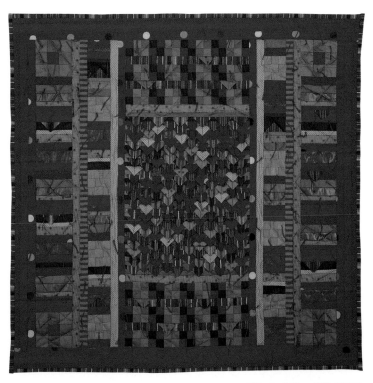

*Carro*, 46" x 46", 1984, private collection

*Polka Dot Fantasy*, 64" x 64", 1984

Although I perceive my work to be very precise and orderly, I do not make mathematically calculated designs. I like to use machine appliqué for the freedom it allows. Sometimes it is fun just to cut up fabrics and see what happens. I was inspired to try this technique myself after seeing a reproduction of a Henri Matisse painting with flowers. I chose bright colors and tried to be spontaneous by cutting directly into the fabrics. For instance, I quickly drew a wisteria flower shape with chalk on a green fabric. Then I freely cut petal shapes from purple fabric, trying to capture the basic flower shapes, and then stitched them to the background green fabrics. For my customary appliqué, I prefer to work by hand. *Still Life With Five Oranges*, worked with the machine, allowed for experimentation. The result is a very colorful piece.

***Still Life With Five Oranges,***
**36" x 28", 1995**

"Red is the great

clarifier—bright,

cleansing, and

revealing. It makes

all other colors

beautiful. I can't

imagine becoming

bored with red—

it would be like

becoming bored

with the person

you love."

Diana Vreeland

*Ah, Red*

1. *Takoage*, (detail)

2. *Homage to a Rainbowmaker*, (detail)

3. *China Doll*, (detail)

4. *Red Jacket*, (detail)

5. *Painted silk patchwork*, (detail)

6. *Masquerade*, (detail)

Throughout the years, one color more than any other has been my favorite. Red was my first favorite, and I used it often in my weavings. Although I do not use red as a dominant part of my work currently, the titles of several pieces reveal its importance to me: *Red Kimono* on page 38, *Red Jacket* on page 32, and *Ah, Red,* an assemblage of items in the color red. Reds and magenta with yellow accents are dominant colors of a woven bag made in the 1970s, and reds, purples, and magenta with green accents details of my patchwork.

*Tibetan Boots*, inspired by boots from Tibet, were hand woven using wool yarn. Rainbow colors descend to the bright yellow felt booties, which have stacked felt in rainbow colors for the soles. Narrow bands of different colors of striped fabric were hand woven to make the fabric needed for *Rainbow Woven Dolls*. In a detail of *China Doll*, see page 57, colors are accentuated with black and white piecing; large prints play off solid-colored fabrics. Even when working with soft pastel silks, color interplay is a strong component of my design. Some would look at the white blossoms of the almond tree as being devoid of color. Quite the opposite, when you notice the contrast of colors in the center of each flower as it lays against the branch.

AS I BEGIN TO WRITE THIS BOOK WE HAVE ELEVEN GRANDCHILDREN. THEIR ages reflect different styles of my quiltmaking through the years. When the first was born, I was proud to make a baby quilt using both patchwork and appliqué, surrounded with black border strips. I remember another quiltmaker asking why I would make a black quilt for a grandchild. I didn't see the quilt as black, but rather as a rainbow.

Thom Klika said, "If the Rainbow came each day do you suppose we'd care? Perhaps we find it beautiful because it is so rare!"

My first grandchild was born when I was still weaving fabrics, and the rainbow was an important part of my weaving color palette. During that time, I also designed needlepoint canvases, and again, I used bright rainbow colors for the designs. Bargello was a familiar needlepoint design to me. I did not know much about quilting patterns, so I thought using the one-inch square in a Bargello pattern would make a good quilt design. The black borders came about as a way to show off the appliqué corner blocks. I mentioned that appliqué was a familiar technique I learned as a child. I wanted to put my best artistic talents into this first quilt. The baby was due between Valentine's Day and Washington's birthday, hence the heart in the upper left corner and three cherries in the lower left corner. This quilt announces my first grandchild with the number one in the upper right corner and the family name, Byrd, that is symbolized in the lower right corner.

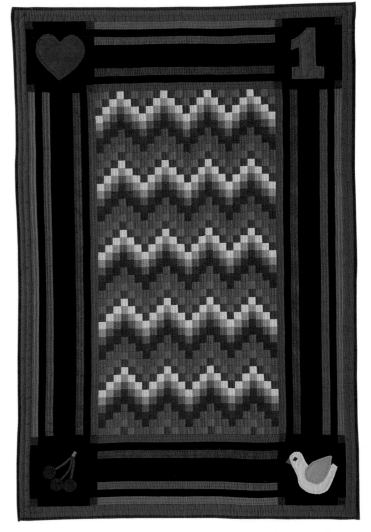

**For Nicholas Joseph,
born 1980**

When I make a quilt for a grand-child, the size is approximately crib size. I do not intend for the child to sleep under the quilt, but prefer that the quilt be hung on a wall. My reason for this is I do not hand quilt using close stitches, and I do not want the quilts to need to be washed. Our children each had a favorite blanket that they carried around the house. I have memories of the trauma when it came time to wash those treasures. As the blankets got older, they were reduced in size and eventually became stuffing for pillows. I could not envision that for the grandchildrens' quilts!

When Vince was five years old he visited my studio, and he asked if I would make him a quilt. A few years before, I had set a small fabric crayon drawing he made in pre-school into a pillow-sized quilt, which he took to bed with him. I mentioned that I had already made him a big quilt and also reminded him of the small one. No, he said, he wanted to help me make another quilt. I gave him my box of strip-pieced scraps and suggested that he could pick out the colors he liked.

Colors which I would not have considered as compatible were perfect for Vince. I suggested that he could help me sew, and he happily helped push the pins into the fabric with my guidance. While at the sewing machine, I carefully stopped stitching so he could pull out the pins, one by one. As the process became boring, he suggested that he would play with the basket of

For Vincent Timothy,
born 1982

wooden spools, and I could call him when the quilt was finished.

Every time he asked if it was finished yet, I would reply that it takes a long time to make a quilt. Finally, after repeated questions, I asked him why he was so impatient. He immediately laid down on the floor with his arms at his sides and said, "So I can try it on to see if it fits." I put the pieced rectangle over his body and it barely covered. When I suggested that it was too small for him, he replied that it was

OK, he wouldn't move.

It was getting time for him to go home, and he wanted to take the quilt with him. I quickly enlarged the backing fabric and folded it over and stitched it to the front. This added a bit of extra width and length.

Off he went with his mother, his new quilt in hand. I secretly hoped no one would see the quilt, because the colors were not what I would have selected. Several months later, his mother said he slept with the new quilt every night.

I was proud to have completed Nick's quilt in plenty of time to give it as a baby shower gift. When the next grandchild was due to arrive, I had not begun the design; however, it was important to me to have the quilt completed before the birth. With three weeks to Delivery Day, I quickly pieced a top using a traditional Amish design that I had seen in a quilt book. Nine Patch to the rescue! The colors of red, purple, and magenta brightened up the design. I could personalize the quilt by quilting motifs of hearts and birds, which conveyed my sentiments.

Log Cabin is a favorite block that I like to use, but I never used the traditional design concept of making blocks in light and dark values to make a full-sized quilt. The idea of stitching strips around a central square is what appeals to me; most of my quilts are based on that principle. I use a pieced block as my square and sew strips in an off-center and irregular pattern, so that the bars are of unequal widths. This method of irregular Log Cabin is the design I selected to use for my next grandson's quilt. I chose bright colors to make the first few blocks and surrounded them with black. Eric's quilt was made after I finished *Snow On Mt. Fuji*, seen on page 43. The red quilting lines on the black fabric show a trio of hearts, signifying this is my third grandchild.

A unique backing for this quilt was made by the oldest two grandsons. I set up a painting space and gave each child white squares of fabric and paint. They enjoyed making colorful "pictures," which I stitched together for the backing.

**For Eric Robert, born 1984**

**For Michael William, born 1986**

In 1989, when it was time to make my next grandchild's quilt, I was continuing to use a diagonal set for my quilts. I still used the irregular Log Cabin concept, but it is practically impossible to identify where the center blocks and the strips are placed. My first four grandsons were born to one family. When the quilts are viewed together, the colors relate in vibrancy and document how my designs have progressed over the six-year period. Each of the quilts has a heart motif that appears in the quilting stitching, and somewhere on the surface there is reference to each grandchild's numerical order of birth.

My interest in quilting and patchwork came from my experience as a weaver and maker of wearable art, as opposed to a background of traditional quilting. During my childhood, the Sunbonnet Sue bedspreads that my mother made for my sister and me covered our beds. When my daughter was young she loved to have these spreads on her twin beds. Some years later, as a remembrance of the old spreads, I made two quilts which included Sunbonnet Sue blocks (circa 1930) that I purchased at an antique shop. Although the blocks were made by someone else, they serve as a reminder of my mother's work.

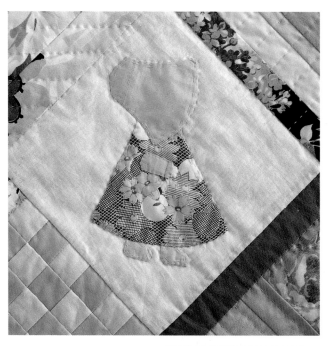

**Sunbonnet Sue block made from 1930s fabric**

*My Mother's Name Was Mary* and *My Father's Name Was Lou* were made and intended as memory quilts to accompany a family quilt, *In Loving Memory*, see page 112. These quilts, which honor my mother and father, were given to my two granddaughters. I wanted to entrust the memories to the granddaughters so that they would be preserved by another generation.

The colors that were used in *My Mother's Name Was Mary* are soft with pale green being the dominant theme. Fabrics were chosen to convey the feeling of the 1930s when my mother was married. There are similar pattern fabrics for *My Father's Name Was Lou*, but the black colors are suggestive of my father's black curly hair and dark flashing eyes. I used to recite a ditty when I was a child…"My mother's name is Mary and my father's name is Lou, and they named my sister Marilou." (I often thought absolutely no one was named Yvonne, and furthermore, you could never buy your initial to wear on a neck chain because they didn't make a "Y." I often queried my family to assure myself that in fact I really did belong.)

**My Mother's Name Was Mary,**
collection of Laura Marie,
born 1988

**My Father's Name Was Lou,**
collection of Elizabeth Jean,
born 1992

When our three sons were living at home, we had one very large bedroom for them with dividing partitions, which provided each son his own space. Through the years I have made curtains for the west windows of this room. After several seasons, the colors would fade and new curtains were made. Once the boys were away at college, it was time to replace the curtains again. When they were home on weekends, I don't think they realized that Mom had covered the windows with a print featuring lace fans and flowers. Time again to replace the curtain fabric. (I managed to salvage the unfaded parts and stored the remainder.) Some years later, when making a quilt for our oldest son's first child, I thought it would be fun to include fabric from one of those bedroom curtains in the quilt.

Medical technology has improved through the years and this time, prior to the event, I knew we were going to have a granddaughter. I selected additional fabrics to complement the special window-curtain floral print and added pink fabrics to honor a female child. I used my traditional heart motif as the center medallion.

**For Vittoria Lee, born 1990**

**For Sarina Yvonne, born 1990**

Two granddaughters born in the same year gave me an opportunity to try similar concepts of floral fabrics and colors, but in a different style. With the second quilt, I included one floral print and the same appliquéd rose used in Vittoria's quilt. The flower represents the idea of giving the quilt as a gift, and Tori's quilt has a "to and from" tag. In Sarina's quilt, the rose is also a remembrance of her mother's favorite flower. Tori's mother likes to scuba dive, hence the fish. In both quilts, the same two small appliquéd hearts represent the parents.

Two more grandchildren and grandma has two more quilts to make. When making Robbie's quilt, I was working on *Six Color World*, and I thought it would be interesting to make a quilt using hand-

**For Robert Louis, born 1995**

painted fabric in conjunction with commercial fabrics. For this quilt the Log Cabin pattern used is an adaptation of Court House Steps. The large center square features a reverse appliquéd heart, and it becomes a medallion around which other fabrics are sewn. The idea behind this quilt was to paint just three quilter's fat quarter-size pieces of fabric and expand that into a large quilt by adding fabrics from my supply on hand. Red, blue, and yellow were the colors for the baby's nursery.

For grandchild number ten I wanted to make a quilt in the same color palette as Robbie's. I used the small amount of painted fabric I had left over from Robbie's quilt to begin the new quilt. I thought it would be fun to use the same style of checkerboard patchwork used for his cousin Sarina, only this time using primary colors.

When pulling fabrics for this quilt I decided that I also wanted to use polka-dot prints as a unifying theme. I began to appliqué circles onto the central appliquéd heart and placed them as needed for the design. When finished, there were exactly ten circles in the central heart, a mere coincidence.

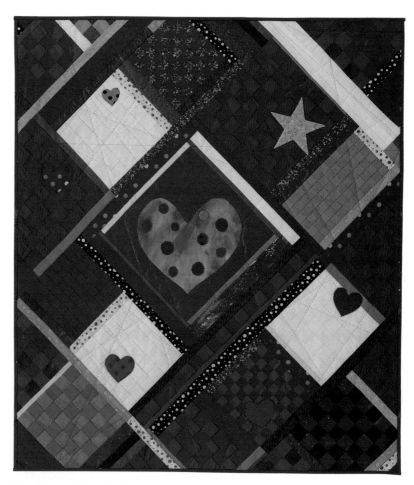

**For Angelo Burtoni Lorenzo,
born 1996**

As I marvel over the beauty of having so many wonderful grandchildren, I think about what it was like when we were raising our four children. Because our children were born within four and a half years of each other it was a very busy time, and sometimes I think of it as a whirlwind passing through my life in one sweeping motion. Recently I met Marianne Fons and Liz Porter at a quilting conference. Many years ago we had shared stories of how we managed children and studio work time. Marianne and Liz reminded me of some of the stories I used to tell during my lectures when I was a beginning artist.

We had built our new country home and added a forty-two-inch-high by twenty-inch-deep counter in the utility room, which would be used for folding laundry. Well, of course everyone knows a mother dumps the clean laundry in the middle of the living room, or at least on a bed, and sorts it that way. If, of course, a guest drops by unexpectedly, seeing this mass of laundry dumped in the middle of the living room only reinforces the concept that you are an overworked mother. I also liked to leave the vacuum cleaner permanently in the middle of the living room, so I could tell my unexpected guest that I was in the middle of house cleaning.

With four little kids running around, I soon learned that cleaning off the kitchen table to use for cutting out garment patterns was not even a remote possibility. I used the laundry utility counter as my sewing table. I developed my method of cutting out small parts of a garment, such as just the bodice or just the sleeves, and set up my sewing machine on the narrow counter. This way, the children could not disrupt the project or touch the dangerous scissors or sharp pins. "Necessity is the Mother of Invention" is the motto, and I learned to sew standing up. Sewing only small sections of a garment at a time and setting small daily goals was very rewarding, and at least I felt that I was being creative. I would stack up all the sewn parts of the garment and then, in one day, I could sew all the pieces together. Magically, I had a finished garment.

Another trick that I had was to buy a box of sugar-coated cereal. I would put the box of cereal on the floor of the playroom where all the children were, and I would retreat to the utility room to sew. When the box of cereal was empty, my sewing time was up. This apparently did not impact upon the development of our children since, when asked, they don't even remember this ploy used by their mother to capture a few quiet minutes. I certainly wouldn't ask them if they were as devious with their own children.

With the birth of another grandchild, we now have six grandsons and five granddaughters. This seemed like a good time to evaluate the types of appliqué and patchwork that I had used over the last eighteen years, and celebrate the number eleven. A trio of calla liles, in the upper left of the quilt, represents a new sister joining the family of our son Greg and his wife, Madhu. Six flowers signify the number of children of our daughter, Suzanne and her husband, Tim. Two lilies honor the children of our son Stephen and his wife, Sandy. I included Checkerboard blocks in this quilt, along with Half Square triangles and narrow strips of my favorite rainbow-colored strip piecing.

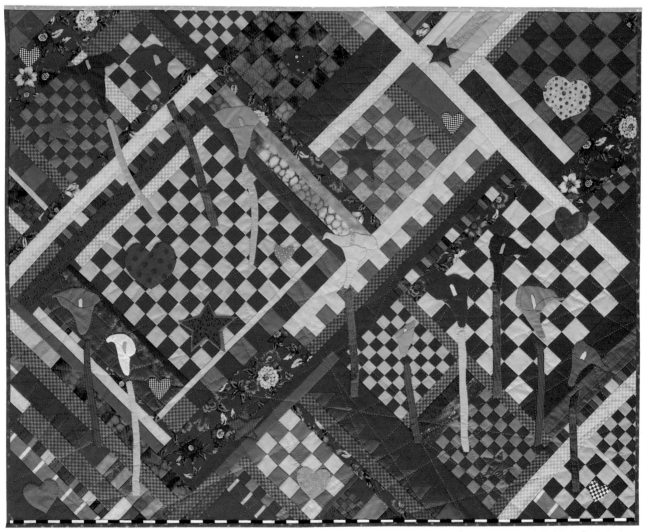

**For Monique Eileen, born 1998**

AMERICANA IS A THEME THAT HAS INTERESTED ME SINCE A 1981 VISIT TO New York City. The trip was arranged so my husband and I might visit the Metropolitan Museum of Art exhibition of Chinese Costumes, as well as the Fashion Institute exhibition of Mariano Fortuny costumes and textiles. Chinese and Italian costumes do not sound very American; it was an incident that happened on the streets of New York that made the trip extraordinary. It had never occurred to me that anyone would actually wear an American flag or a shirt that represented the designs of the flag. As we were walking along enjoying the sights of New York, a patron of a hot-dog vendor moved into my field of vision. I snapped a picture of her, and to this day, I can remember exactly the feeling that I experienced, not only a "Kodak® moment," but a "stick it back into the memory bank moment." After that experience, working with Americana images became a goal.

My good friend Maggie Brosnan knew of my interest in capturing sponta-
neous Americana images. She is the photographer credited with taking the photo of the "Spirits of America" quick stop market. Maggie epitomized a generous spirit who had a humorous outlook on life and art. She was an inspiration just being herself, which reflected in the lives of her friends and students. Maggie taught design and fiber arts at local community colleges in the Silicon Valley of California. Even though she lived a two-hour drive away from me, we saw each other often. Our first meeting, in 1971, was at the opening of an art center where I was demonstrating hand spinning. She came and sat on the floor next to me, and we discussed the process necessary to control a spinning wheel while making a fine thread. For the next twenty-three years we celebrated creativity together.

**Spirits of America, Chico, CA.**

Left: **Hot Dogs and more;
New York City**

73

Windup toys, plastic flowers, and even an eight-legged camel were "Maggie Material." Everything was considered artist materials in her world. A crushed bottle cap on the road was picked up and tucked away for a future collage. Long before it was popular, she began an impressive collection of the world's most unusual, and some would say tacky, rhinestone jewelry. Each piece was stored in a cellophane bag and safely placed in a beautiful Tansu (a Japanese-style chest). Buttons and plastic beads found their way into her art, and soon her studio was filled with an assortment of trinkets, each stored by color in clear plastic boxes. When making necklaces from these, she dispensed the color sequences into disposable plastic cookie trays, but when first sorting her newly acquired buttons, she used an antique African grain basket. Guests at parties in her home would eventually get around to playing with her collection of tin windup toys. Her collection of favorite recipes served as gifts to friends, each page handwritten in her perfect script. I am not sure why, but Maggie had selected color names for herself and her friends. Her name was "Pink" and she called me "Magenta."

One day I received a large envelope that contained a color copy of one of Maggie's collages, this one featuring pink candy wrappers. On the back of the page was a letter. The following message was printed with rubber stamps in red ink: DEAR YVONNE, PLEASE SEND ME THE FOLLOWING FOR MY SHRINES: 2 DOZEN "PASHA" POSTCARDS, A PHOTO OF STEVE, YOU, AND ME WITH STEVE IN THE MIDDLE SMILING, THE WRAPPER OF YOUR FAVORITE CANDY BAR, ANOTHER PHOTO OF THE THREE OF US, A FOLDED DOLLAR BILL, YOUR FAVORITE WORD, THE NAMES OF YOUR KITTIES, THE DATE OF YOUR TRIP TO JAPAN, AN OLD VALENTINE, THE NAME OF SUZANNE'S BABY TO BE, THE NAME OF YOUR FAVORITE FLOWER, A TINY PIECE OF LACE, AND 3 BUTTONS. HAPPY VALENTINE'S DAY. senorita pink.

At that time, making shrines was Maggie's *oeuvre*. The idea originated when, as a teacher, she received gifts at the end of the semester from her students. The gifts given to her were usually pink, and they found their way into or onto a living room wall "shrine to pink" (the color pink). During the tenure of the shrine it was moved to the Palo Alto Cultural Center for an art exhibition. Comments registered by those attending the show were generally all the same..."Oh, my God..." Everything in the altar was pink: gum wrappers, cans of food with pink labels, plastic toys, plastic flowers, bits of yarn, an apron, a doll, a heart-shaped valentine box, and on and on.

**Correspondence from "Pink" with shrine components.**

My family was truly surprised when, for my birthday, Maggie gifted me with a shrine. Large enough to make a serious art statement, it was difficult to find a suitable place to hang the installation. Our children had all moved away from home, and upon receiving the shrine, the most appropriate place to hang it seemed to be the deserted "children's" bathroom. (We didn't lose four children, instead we gained a spare bathroom.) For many years this room became the repository of items suitable for enshrinement. Visitors to our home would first be taken to this water closet to enjoy the artistic experience. If they didn't bolt out the door, they usually remained friends.

During the Australian bicentennial in 1988, I was invited to teach there for one month. It was important for me to take something to work on to prevent quilter's withdrawal—being denied fabric, needle, and thread. In the evening after class, I could have some handwork to do. I chose to design appliqué panels based on some of the tacky things Maggie and I had exchanged as gifts. The finished panels could then be set with strip piecing into a quilt. When selecting the colors for the quilt, chartreuse seemed like a good place to begin. The problem of finding perfect chartreuse green prints to accompany the design concept was not an easy task. I selected other colors, and finally, with the help of a group of quilters in Southern California, obtained a few 1960 vintage chartreuse prints.

**Shrine made by Maggie Brosnan,** originally made to hang on the wall, is shown here on a pedestal with her silk tie-dye fabric.

Hidden in the shrine are some of the treasured items requested in Maggie's correspondence.

The first appliqué designed was the eight-legged camel, and others followed, each representing American themes or iconography. The camel was, and still is, a battery operated toy. Made of tin and plastic, the camel has a compartment for two large batteries. Turn the switch to "on" and the camel walks using eight legs, or rather, it lumbers across a surface, crossing anything in its path. When conversation lulls during a dinner party, a show stopper is to bring out the camel and enjoy a race during coffee and dessert.

The yellow chick, an Easter gift for Maggie and one for me, is for the dispensing of jelly beans; fill the body with colorful candy beans, press down on the top of the head, and suddenly a jelly bean drops between the legs. Such a ridiculous item was a perfect gift to add to the collection and another design to add to the quilt.

The red plastic fish, which is actually a container, can be opened and filled with any small item. This too was a gift from Maggie, and I have used it many times as a design for appliqué. Can you find the fish in this quilt? See *California Postcard* on page 106, where Sunbonnet Sue has the fish on a leash and is taking it for a walk.

In 1989, the Great American Gallery in Atlanta suggested I invite artists to participate in an exhibition entitled *Americana Enshrined*. Gallery owners Pat and Martha Connell shared my interest in organizing a quilt exhibition that reflected the Americana theme. Each quilt would either, by the content or shape, enshrine a symbol of America. As an example, two artists chose to use baseball as a theme; one quilt enshrines a famous baseball player and the other refers to the baseball diamond as a cathedral. Another artist used the theme of beauty pageant, another the human "rat race," another the decorative calendar. The inventiveness of each of the invited artists (Sally Broadwell, Kay Burlingham, Jane Burch Cochran, Nancy Crow, Chris Wolf Edmonds, Nancy Erickson, Holley Junker, Edward Larsen, Therese May, Susan Shie, and Judi Warren) was outstanding. Their personal correspondence during the development of the show also reflected their unique individuality of design. Many artists sent small drawings; one artist attached bits of colored fabrics to her letter. Often the envelopes were decorated with unique artistic designs. Many of these items were photographed and included in the show catalog. Statements offered by each artist gave insight into their creative processes.

At the time it seemed to me that everywhere I looked were bumper stickers that proclaimed, with a red heart, the love of just about anything. "I ♥" my dog, my car, Elvis, Graceland, and so on. My quilt for the *Americana Enshrined* exhibition immortalized that famous red heart. The large heart is filled with images that have become icons of America: Mickey Mouse® is certainly the most famous. The cactus suggests the impact in home decor of anything representing the southwest, which in 1989 was all the rage. At the time when I made the quilt, the dancing raisin advertising campaign was in full swing to promote the California raisin industry. I found the image on a twin bed sheet, which I cut up to use the motif. When looking for icon images printed on fabric, sometimes you have to be satisfied with any kind of fabric! Flowers in a variety of containers offer homage to the heart, but also suggest that this might be the funeral for the "I red heart" motto. The can of spinach, seen on page 81, is a veiled reference to a popular icon of my youth. I remember the hidden agenda of that cartoon, which was to encourage young children to eat their spinach so they could grow to be strong.

Often times I will repeat an image in a series of quilts. This gives continuity to a theme and also represents my devotion to a specific remembrance. My maternal grandmother's name was Rose. During the late 1980s, I often used an appliquéd rose image as a reminder of her. I never fancied myself a gardener; I was fortunate to live on a ranch where the trees bloomed every year without my nurturing. I always wanted to grow roses but somehow never found the time. Arranging fabric roses on a quilt is a personal satisfaction.

***Americana Enshrined,
36" x 38", 1989,*** catalog
cover quilt

**Detail of *I ♥ America***

At one time, I thought I should make one giant rose to get the image out of my system. In 1989, I was recovering from my knee surgery and had to sit with my leg elevated. Handwork seemed the perfect solution to being stuck in one spot. I thought of the rose as being served up on a platter. I enlarged my rose pattern and put it on a background of black and white checkerboard fabric. The surrounding fabric suggests the rim of the platter and is filled with chili peppers. In 1993, I reworked the quilt and added even more roses to the border. I guess I will never tire of using the rose image!

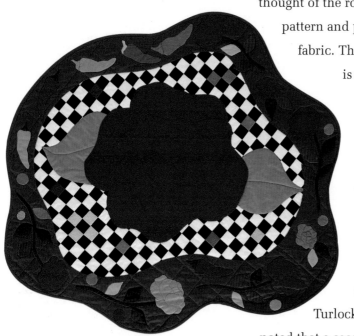

**The New Rose, 40" x 49",
1989,** reworked in 1993

In 1992, several newspaper articles caught my attention. Theme parks and fast food restaurants were being built in Europe and Japan; we were now exporting American-style food and family entertainment. Closer to home, the town of Turlock is the site of the California State University at Stanislaus, sometimes referred to as Turkey Tech. Turkey farms are a major industry in Turlock, as well as parts of Stanislaus County. The newspaper noted that a secondary industry has developed to recycle the turkey feathers. Not only are the feathers collected and cleaned, but there is a market for them. It is interesting to note that the feathers can be dyed and used in fashion items, such as to decorate a hat or make a feather boa. Some feathers from Turlock are dyed yellow and find their way into bird costumes. My interest in American themes and shrines was fueled by this interesting information.

The theme "America's Greatest Hits" asks the question, just what is representative of America to our foreign visitors? What are the important tourist destinations? What items do they want to take home with them, or which experiences are important while they are here? Why do people want to eat our style of food even when they are in their own country? My thoughts turned to images of a hamburger, an ice cream cone, a pink flamingo, a "no smoking" sign, a cowboy boot, and my favorite, 99¢.

Another very popular American image, possibly not recognized by foreign visitors, is the ever present flowerpot filled with a ubiquitous philodendron, which is that trailing vine found in so many homes, half dead, but too difficult to throw away. Several years ago, my son Don accompanied me to The Big Apple, New York City. We had great fun doing the tourist things—taking pictures from the top of the Empire State Building and walking the length of Manhattan from SoHo to Central

Park. I thought it would be fun to have a luxurious meal at the Polo Club Restaurant on Madison Avenue. It was very posh, with tuxedo-clad waiters, white tablecloths, fine china, and large bouquets of beautifully arranged flowers everywhere. Two days later, when we were staying in a Long Island motel, I pointed out the reality of our surroundings to my son. While having dinner at the motel restaurant, not only was the yellow bucket and floor mop parked adjacent to our table, but a color-less philodendron plant was struggling to survive in a water-filled wine carafe that was perched on the booth divider. What is it about this plant that prevents it from being replaced? Is this what defines an icon?

## In Praise of a Life

On the same occasion as the gifting of Maggie's shrine to me, she also arranged a picnic tour of the cemeteries in and around San Francisco as a birthday celebration. This interest in cemeteries originates not in the macabre but in finding wonderful imagery. A particular interest I have is photographing monuments that have the index finger extended, right hand pointing upward. I had previously photographed a local cemetery during a trip to Gatlinburg, Tennessee, which was the circumstance for my finding "Jesus Called." A longtime interest of mine has been documenting the eclectic, yet sentimental, floral arrangements and remembrances left at grave sites. I do not intend to offend, but rather, join other photographers who memo-rialize these images. The cemetery above the town of Gatlinburg, gateway to the Smoky Mountains, is nestled among trees on a steep hill behind the commercial strip of local shops. The diminished colors on weathered floral arrangements that had survived the winter snows caught my eye. One very special arrangement stood out among the rest. There upon a Styrofoam® base was a plastic toy phone, with lettering on it indicating that Jesus called.

**Gone But Not Forgotten,
70" x 63", 1989**

1.  **Pigeon Forge, Tennessee, 1987**
2.  **Another Angel**
3.  **Jesus Called**
4.  **Pet Cemetery, Presidio, San Francisco**
5.  **Presidio overview**
6.  **Angel statuary; Colma, California**
7.  **Mr. Twister; Presidio, San Francisco, 1990**
8.  **Chinese Cemetery; Colma, California**
9.  **Raspberry; Presidio, San Francisco, 1987**

**Green Glass and Empties,**
**61" x 45", 1989**

Right: ***Too Pink, Goodbye Angel,***
**24" x 23", 1994**

An article had appeared in a San Francisco newspaper describing the resting places for pets in that city. Upon seeing this, Maggie suggested that we make an event out of our visit, perhaps a birthday picnic among the tombstones. Tucked under the overpass of a local freeway on the grounds of the Presidio, a U.S. Army base, we found a well-tended cemetery. This is the final resting place for the remains of family pets owned by the military and their dependents. On the day we visited, I took photographs, and I have since returned several times to document my experiences. During the past twelve years, I have witnessed changes from meticulous conservation to rampant destruction. After the 1989 Bay Area earthquake, it has been necessary to retrofit many of the San Francisco freeway overpasses. Retrofitting the overpass that is over the pet cemetery determined the fate of many of the graves. Now the government has relinquished control of the Presidio to state and private development that will further jeopardize the site.

When I was very young, funerals were a part of life. As a family we attended many to honor friends or relatives. Later, as a member of the church choir, I sang at many religious services.

My grandfather, who died when I was two years old, was interred in the local cemetery; the size of the crypt seemed very large in the eyes of a child. Old family photographs of him showed a large robust man with a kind smile. *Green Glass and Empties* remembers the family crypt and also honors the eclectic assortment of flowers and containers left at grave sites. I also made a quilt to honor our family pets as well as those who remain at the Presidio, and after the untimely death of Maggie Brosnan, I made a small quilt to honor her memory.

Political quilts also qualify for my Americana theme. When I make a political quilt, it is not blatant in its design, but rather, subtle. During the 1991 Gulf War, many artists made quilts as a way of understanding this crisis. When I began my design, I selected six hearts, corresponding to the number of grandchildren we had at the time. My concern was that if old enough to serve, which "heart" would be sent to war? The severe tapered point of the shape of each heart contrasts my previously used heart shapes found on the grandchildren's quilts, which feature a rounded design. The stars are reminders of our flag, and the yellow binding exemplifies the yellow ribbons worn to honor those enlisted to fight.

Made to honor the children lost during the Oklahoma City bombing.

*On Wednesday Morning,*
**70" x 50", 1995,** shown in
*Sewing Comfort Out Of Grief,*
sponsored by the Helias
Foundation

Left: *February,* **60" x 46",
1991**

7

# THE FIGURE QUILTS:

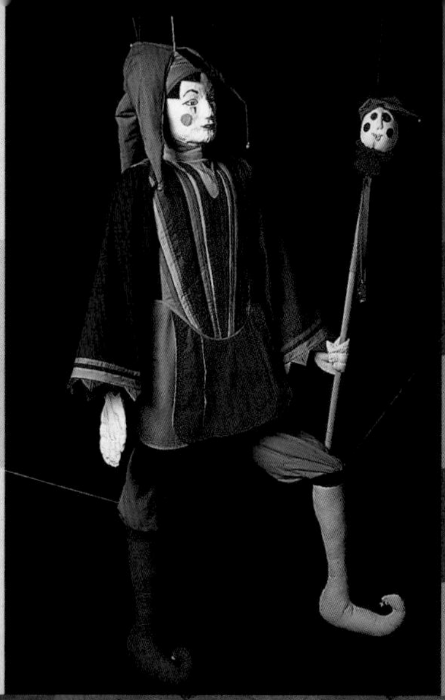

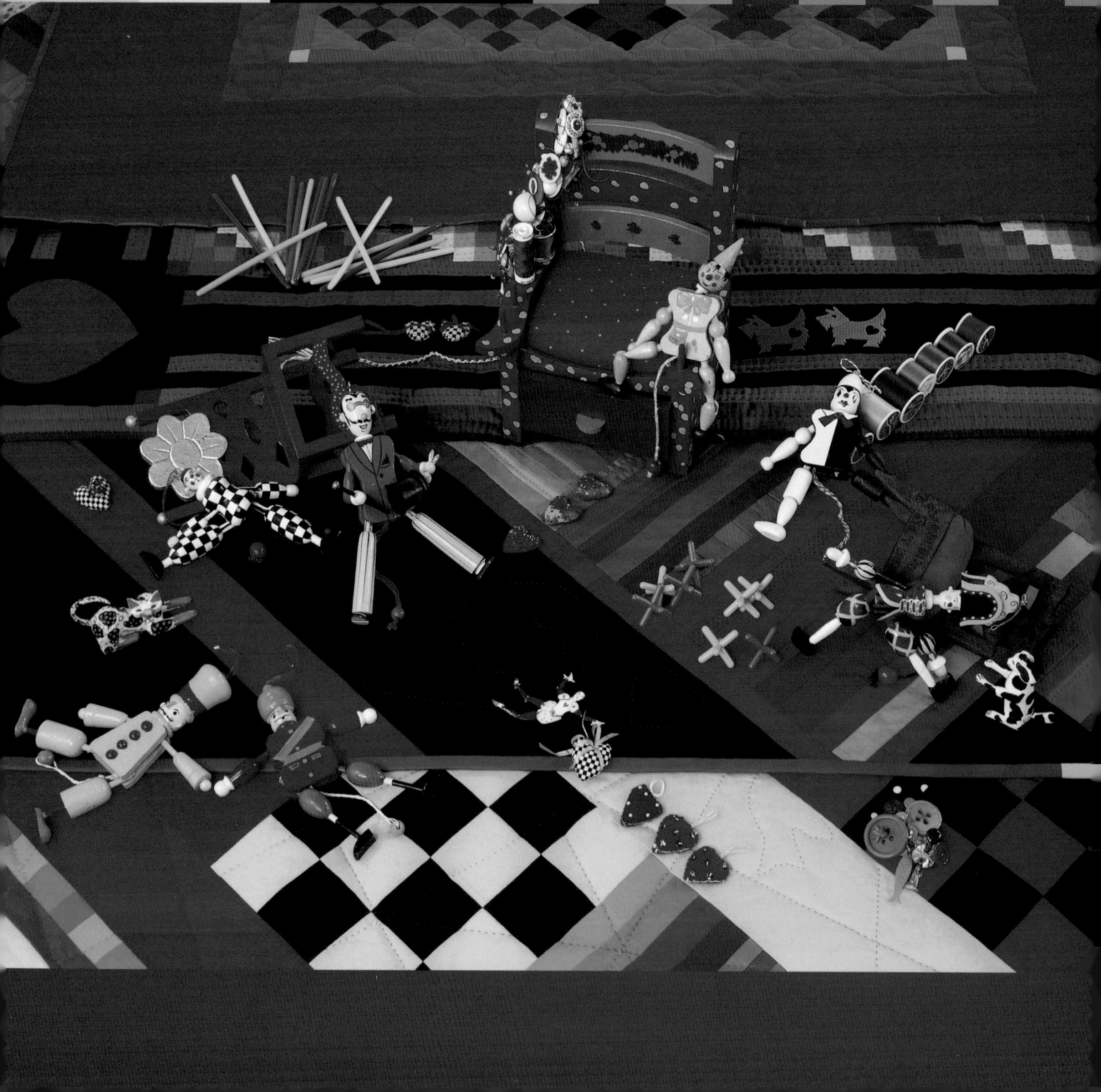

WHEN MY SISTER AND I WERE VERY YOUNG, WE HAD A DOLL COLLECTION. For special occasions the usual gift was a doll, and at one time we had the complete collection of the popular Nancy Ann Storybook Dolls. Family friends who traveled the world also brought us dolls dressed in native costumes. My mother very diligently wrote each name of the doll, the benefactor, and occasion and date for which it was given in a memory book. We were never allowed to play with these dolls, but each was examined to note the completeness of costume and construction of the body. The collection is still intact. The dolls have suffered slightly from years of storage in the attic, but each has a sentimentality that is overwhelming. Matching up the doll with the giver by reading the gift book brings back old memories. Now the collection belongs to granddaughters, and they too only look at the dolls through the glass case.

Did you ever make paper dolls that had fasteners at the knees, elbows, and shoulders so the paper doll could move? I remember playing with those dolls, and today, I still have a small round box of forty brass paper fasteners, the kind used to joint the doll. Simple in concept, these paper dolls could be cut from plain or decorated colored papers. I remember being fascinated with the articulation of the movements, which are limited yet magical. Wooden dolls that have a string attached to arms and legs (the doll makes only one quick motion of extended arms and legs by pulling the string) are another personal fascination. These two types of dolls, paper and wooden, serve as the inspiration for making quilts which celebrate the articulating figure.

**Hector** and author, 1980

Facing page, top: **Hector with jester stick**

Perhaps the best place to begin my contemporary doll odyssey would be to review why, in 1975, I made a cloth doll that stood almost six feet tall. At that time I was weaving fabrics while making wearable art and designing garment patterns. For that year's annual weavers conference I wove narrow bands of cotton from which I made three eleven-inch-high dolls. (See the woven bands on page 12 with one of the dolls.) I was asked to design the display booth for the rainbow colored items that were submitted by the local guild members. Using the concept of dolls, I made *Hector*, the puppet who was to be central to the decor of the booth. He was displayed in a position of exuberance, supported by the display booth's upright poles.

The doll is definitely not anatomically correct (since I am a nursing school graduate, I can confirm that certain pertinent body features are absent). To begin the doll, I made the patchwork shirt. I stuffed a turtleneck sweater with a pillow, filled the neck and arms with additional stuffing, and put the shirt on. I used white muslin for the hands and stitched them on at the sleeve cuffs. The head is a stuffed football shape that I stitched to the turtleneck band. I made a papier-mâché mask and tied it onto the head; the jester hat was stitched to the top of the head. I stuffed the pants to form the lower body and then attached the lower legs. For many years after the 1975 weavers conference, *Hector* traveled in the passenger seat of my car, acting, for all to see, as my companion during the times I drove home alone after giving an evening lecture.

In 1989, after sewing the last seam to stitch the binding on a ten-foot commissioned pieced-and-quilted wallhanging, I got up from my sewing machine to iron. I could picture myself ironing, but amazingly, my mind was faster than my body. I stood up from the machine with one leg at an angle and tore the cartilage in my knee. I subsequently had arthroscopic knee surgery. Due to previous damage to the knee and the swelling and pain, standing for any period of time was uncomfortable. Physical therapy provided the solution to the problem, but also enlightened me to the concept of "use it or lose it." In the past "pumping iron" in my vocabulary referred to moving that iron that is plugged into the wall, with a point at one end and holes in the bottom that spit steam. Sitting with all the other "knee patients" in the large physical therapy treatment room, I had the opportunity to watch other injured patients perform anatomically specific exercises. Suddenly I realized that if movement was important to me (certainly more than the articulation of a paper doll), I had to make exercise a part of my life. The design for *Keep Both Feet On The Floor* was inspired by my indoctrination into the world of exercise.

*Keep Both Feet On The Floor*, 77" x 54", 1990

*Oh, What A Feeling*, 68" x 48", 1991

I used a paper doll as the inspiration for a pattern. First I cut rectangular panels and added the limited motion figure in appliqué. Each figure is slightly different, and the large figure at the top portrays a figure falling. After stitching the appliqué blocks, I added strip piecing to each block and sewed these into the quilt top.

The theme of the quilt is the body in motion, but the title of the quilt actually comes from another event. During a trip to Tennessee, while riding the trolley from the parking lot to the entrance of the Dollywood Theme Park in Pigeon Forge, the driver's announcement sparked the idea for the title. When all the passengers had filled the empty seats, we heard the driver proclaim, "This trolley will not move unless everyone keeps both feet on the floor and all body parts inside." In my quilt, keeping your feet on the floor might suggest that you are inactive when in fact movement is the answer.

Using the same paper doll appliqué pattern, I designed a second quilt, *Oh, What A Feeling*. Each figure was stitched using colorful fabrics to suggest a circus costume. I wanted to test the figure in limited motion by restricting the size of the individual blocks to a narrow format.

Another favorite theme used in this quilt is the chili pepper. I also used chilies in *Riding An 8 Legged Camel*, seen on page 77. Santa Fe, New Mexico, a haven of artists with its beautiful natural colors and fantastic vistas, is a favorite tourist destination. In late November I was invited to teach in Santa Fe, and I noticed strings of decorative lights that had red or green plastic chili peppers covering tiny, white light bulbs were artfully hung throughout the city and its businesses. And when ordering a taco at a restaurant the waitress asked, "White or blue corn meal?" and then, "Red or green chili?" Not only was Santa Fe inspiration by itself, but colored taco shells and different colored chili peppers gave me food for thought. In subsequent quilts, I used the chili form in many colors, and sometimes the chili is included next to my other favorite design, the lily.

Inspiration to make the next quilt in this series featuring the figure came while watching the televised Olympic gymnastic trials. This event was one of the many trials before the athletes are chosen to represent their country in the next Olympic Games. It seemed that the important part of the competition was the scores. After each trial the gymnast would approach the coach, receive a hug, and then both would surreptitiously look for the scoreboard numbers. This gave the impression that success alone was very important; there was no excuse for failure.

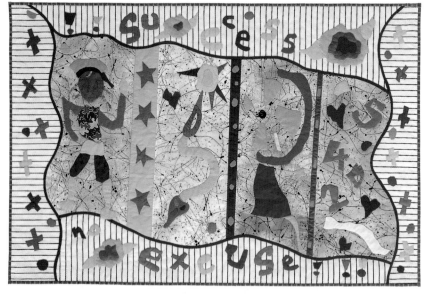

*Success*, 45" x 68", 1992

To make my quilt, I first drew a small sketch with the surface of the quilt divided into four sections, each representing a different part of the event. The figure in the first panel honors the universal athlete, sort of a generic person outfitted in workout clothes. The second panel is fictitious, but suggests pieces or parts of various exercise equipment that might be part of the athletes' training regime. Panel three honors the fans who sit and enjoy watching the trials or event. The fourth panel honors the importance of numbers, as well as the cardiovascular benefits of exercise on the heart, and there is a small remnant of a towel, very important for sweat control. Surrounding these images, the quilt borders feature the hugs, kisses, and flowers suggestive of success.

*Arnold*, 45" x 45", 1994

For twenty-five years, our home was the almond ranch in Modesto. When the children left to enjoy their careers, my husband and I were suddenly faced with not only a large home, but also a diminished workforce. For many years, care of the property was shared by the whole family, and now it reverted back to just the two of us. Although retirement did not seem imminent, we decided to invest in a place for the future. An area of remoteness and breathtaking beauty, the Sierra Nevada mountains had been our family vacation destination for many years. This seemed like a good spot to begin our search for a second home.

Backpacking trips as family vacations began when our oldest son could carry a small pack. As each child reached that stage, one at a time, each of our four children were added to the trail. There was no room for luxuries; food was minimal, clothes and bedding were what you could carry. Being in the wilderness, walking for miles with a pack on your back, sleeping in a tent on the ground, and cooking over a small fire, although exhilarating, was a working vacation. The end of the trip, getting back to the car, was always cause for celebration. Entering back into civilization called for a reward; we would stop for a real meal in one of the small towns that sheltered the trailheads. Because getting to the remoteness of the mountains was our focus, it never occurred to us that one of these small towns might be a possible place to live, with more to it than just the local eateries.

We selected a spot and our decision to move was made. The home was purchased, family possessions sorted—many left behind, many misplaced—and many replaced into new surroundings. A new small studio was arranged for me, and I set out to make a new quilt there to convince myself that creativity moved with me, and it was not determined by the view out the window or the size of the room.

Arnold is the name of the town where we selected this new house. Actually we divided home into two places, a patio home in Modesto, to be used as a residence while we were still working, and a home for future retirement in Arnold. Most of our treasures were moved to Arnold with the thought that if our favorite possessions were there, we would want to go there. If filled with castoffs, the new home would not be appealing nor seem like our special place.

**Calaveras Big Trees State Park, California**

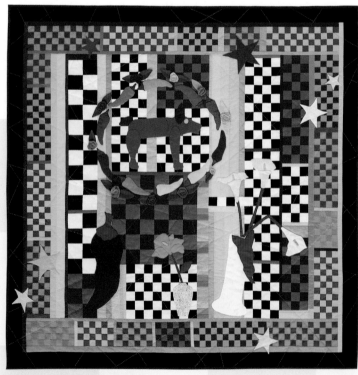

After moving to our new home in Arnold, located just three miles from an old-growth forest with a grove of giant sequoia trees, I wanted to make a new quilt reflective of living in a new environment. The *Arnold* quilt shows my paper doll figure in a new configuration. Instead of a static figure with limited motion, Arnold is both the figure and represents the move. A move from a long-term residence can be a trying experience. The image here is suggestive of being disconnected. I traded almond trees for pine trees (but realistic nature images have never appeared in my quilts). Other quilts which have a similar figure as the central theme are *Arnold Meets The Purple Dog* shown in the road series on page 109, and *Time Master*, which appears on page 131.

## The Purple Dog and The Frog:
### Finding The Purple Dog

The following quilts expand on the concept of the figure, animal rather than human, with a simplified version of the same design principles of head, body, and legs, with the addition of the tail and ears.

*And Then Termites Ate The Purple Dog* honors the memory of a little, wooden carved figure of a purple painted dog from Oaxaca, Mexico. When designing the funeral piece for the dog, I selected a wreath of multicolored chili peppers

**And Then Termites Ate The Purple Dog, 61" x 61", 1990**

During the years when I was weaving and investing in historical textiles, my interest in folk costumes also awakened an awareness in the art forms of other cultures. I am fascinated by the sculpture made by artists from inaccessible or remote areas of the world. It suggests to me the inherent human need to be creative, even if the medium at hand is clay from a streambed or a log from a nearby forest. Sometimes the sculpture reflects similar decorative elements

found in the regional textiles. History informs us that investigation into other art forms was popular and influenced many artists of the twentieth century. Today, as we end this century and witness global communication, it is rare to not be knowledgeable about art from every part of the world.

The hand-woven and embroidered costumes worn by women and men in Mexico and Guatemala are colorful and intricate in design. In Oaxaca, Mexico, the villagers carve figures of fantasy animals, some of which have highly decorative surfaces. Other artists make figures that are simpler in appearance but equally beautiful. One such figurine, that of a six-inch-high carved wooden dog, painted purple and decorated with black polka-dotted yellow ears and a white tail, made its way into my collection. The purple dog was crudely carved, with legs and ears nailed into place. I purchased the purple dog and put him atop an antique Japanese Tansu with other disparate treasures. Looking at the funny shaped purple dog one day, I was inspired to make a pattern for appliqué, which found its way into many future quilts. A few months later, while dusting the top of the persimmon wood Tansu, I noticed piles of sawdust that corresponded to the position of the feet of the purple dog. The purple dog had brought resident vermin with him that were eating the soft wood of his legs. Repeated attempts to kill the pests finally resulted in the demise of the purple dog. A concern was that the pests might infest other wooden items in our wooden house. Although memorialized in my quilts with different colors and configurations, I still look in ethnic arts shops for another purple dog, and I have begun to collect a few decorative purple dogs in an attempt to find the perfect replacement.

*Chili, Purple Dog, Chili Chili,*
72" x 61 ¹/₂", 1990

to encircle the purple dog; lilies also decorate the quilt. Of course, I am aware that the pests that were eating the wooden legs of the dog figure were not termites. My thoughts when choosing the title were about termite infestation being universal, and there was a possibility then that termites imported from Mexico could have eaten him. I did not think it made for a descriptive enough title to substitute for accuracy, "Wood bores ate my purple dog!"

Another version of the purple dog quilt series has a subtle reminder of the now-buried purple dog. Using predominately red colors, this quilt suggests the warm or even hot taste of some red and green chili peppers. I enlarged the appliqué dog pattern and used it as one of the quilting designs. On close inspection of the quilt, you can see the faint outline of the purple dog.

Through the years we have had our share of family pets. It seems that most people remember names of their pets and have fond memories surrounding the time and place of cohabitation, including the time of separation. Many of our departed family pets were ceremoniously buried as a means of closure for the children. It occurred to me that a paradise for pets might be the fantasy place where dogs and cats go to play after their earthly time is over. This is the place where dogs chase milk bones across the night sky, and cats dream of an unending supply of fish.

**Pet Paradise, 44" x 60",
1992,** private collection

*If I Could Make A Glass
Dog Bark*, 34" x 52", 1994

I heard a phrase one day, "if I could make a glass dog bark," and I wondered what that would mean. After some thought, another quilt developed in the pet paradise series. There is a magical place that we humans know nothing about where the fantasy dog takes on many different colors.

I asked a good friend of mine if he knew why there was currently such an interest in angels. There are stores that feature angel gifts, books about angels have become popular, and family television programs glamorize stories about angels. His answer was that it had to do with the coming of the end of the twentieth century. People are looking to the spiritual now, just as was done at the end of the last century. This seemed like a good theme for a small quilt: a place where everyone has wings.

**Dog, Frog, and Cherub, 32" x 20", 1995,** private collection

## 8

THE ROAD SERIES:

WHEN REQUESTS CAME FOR TEACHING ASSIGNMENTS IN OTHER PARTS OF the world, they provided me with not only inspirational vistas, but also the unique opportunity to meet other quilt artists and share ideas. Fabrics and colors brought into the classroom, whether in another state or far-distant country, are surprisingly similar today, compared to what was common when I began teaching. This universality of quiltmaking today is due in part to the itinerant teachers, who have introduced, by personal example, the traditions from their worlds. We live in a global village; inspirations, patterns, and books, as well as supplies, are available almost anywhere you live.

My road series of quilts are influenced by travel experiences, but they are not made to reflect a single event or contain that one special piece of fabric found on the trip. Familiar imagery, or perhaps a unique color combination, sparks the ideas and these are integrated into many quilts.

The facade of a welding shop on the corner of Hart Road and Highway 132 greeted me every time my travels took me to distant horizons. I had to turn left or right onto the main road at this spot; waiting for traffic to pass gave pause to enjoy the view across the road. Corrugated metal siding served as a canvas for the painter who decorated the building. Although primitive in execution, the design reminded me of a quilt. Now painted over, the gray-colored building currently holds no artistic interest, but the fond memory remains.

In 1987, fellow quilt teacher Katie Pasquini Masopust and I were traveling across upstate New York in a rental car when we became slightly lost. Eventually we found our way to Niagara Falls and then back to the "Quilting By The Lake" residence hall, but a road sign remains an inspirational patchwork memory.

1. **Kyoto, Japan; Shrine iris garden**
2. **Hiroshima, Japan, students at International Peace Center**
3. **Mediterranean, Italy; waters edge**
4. **Fushimi Inari, Japan, shrine**
5. **Arles, France; marble floor tile**
6. **Hiroshima, Japan, dinner**
7. **Nordkirken, Germany; alley of trees at school**
8. **California pine needles**
9. **Bleu Printer, Germany**
10. **Chicago; Chagall mosaic wall**
11. **Arles, France; Ancient Sarcophagi**

Why a pink pig was parked in the car lot next to the Modesto Banking Company is unknown. I was not aware of any recent parade or event generating the need for such creativity. Having noticed it on a Sunday, I returned the next day with my camera. The pink pig was still there, again without explanation. The picture is worth a thousand words. I like to refer to this as the perfect pink paper pig in the parking lot, but could it be just a Piggy Bank?

In Modesto, as in many of the towns in the San Joaquin valley, there is an arch decorating what was at one time the main entrance to the town. These two-sided welcoming arches proclaim the name of the town, and some are illuminated so they

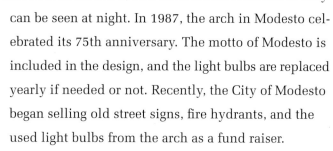

can be seen at night. In 1987, the arch in Modesto celebrated its 75th anniversary. The motto of Modesto is included in the design, and the light bulbs are replaced yearly if needed or not. Recently, the City of Modesto began selling old street signs, fire hydrants, and the used light bulbs from the arch as a fund raiser.

Familiar to Watsonville gardens is the kniphofia plant (its common name is red hot poker), that shares the same space with the calla lily. As my world opened up with travel, I found this favorite childhood lily in many other cities.

In 1986 I published *A Colorful Book*, which was to serve as a record of my work up to that time. The intent of the book was to make a colorful presentation of my garments and quilts without text, just pictures. At that time, color was my starting point and I experimented with simple quilt blocks set in a modified Log Cabin pattern or strip piecing. Upon completion of the book, I faced the dilemma of what I should do next, what designs to use for future quilts. It felt like my whole life was contained between the front and back covers of a 120-page book.

After 1986, a new style emerged where I began to place personal or recognizable images in quilts and surrounded these squares or rectangles with colorful strips. Sometimes the images were cut from printed fabrics, sometimes they were hand

drawn, or were images transferred from photographs.

Rather than depend only on the interplay of color, content now entered my quilts. I wanted my new style to incorporate images, tell a story, and use the theme of travel. The first quilt in this style would celebrate the immigration and visitation of people to

*Taking The Greyhound To
Bakersfield*, 75" x 71", 1986

The back side of *Taking The
Greyhound To Bakersfield*

After I returned from Japan, where *A Colorful Book* was printed, the first quilt that I made was not a quilt inspired by the natural beauty of that country, but rather a quilt about an event taking place in California. The Pope, Vicar of the Catholic Church, was visiting the United States, including California, in 1986. This event was orchestrated by large cities to enable thousands of the faithful to see the Pontiff with a minimum of disruption to the local communities. The solution was that everyone would have to take chartered buses from local churches to a central location. Buses, once parked, would disgorge the passengers, who would sit in bleachers to view the ceremonies. Each parish was assigned a section of the stadium so all could view the Pope from a distance. I stayed home to watch it on television and made a quilt!

Long before the Pope was scheduled to come to America, Nancy Halpern, who is a friend as well as a traveling quilt teacher, received a specialty fabric that had been printed in Cameroon from one of her students. It was the ultimate, "what do you do with this piece of fabric" challenge. Nancy's solution was to send the fabric to me. I kept it on my shelf for many years. Now was the time to utilize this celebratory fabric printed in Cameroon, when the Pope visited that country.

Because this quilt was going to appear in my travel series, I reflected on the thought that at the far end of the longest valley in California lies the town of Bakersfield. From Bakersfield you leave the valley to climb over the Tehachapi Mountains and enter the Los Angeles basin. The great, or Big Valley, as it has been called, is 500 miles long and includes the Sacramento and San Joaquin valleys. The Sierra Nevada mountains form the majestic east border. The climate is temperate most of the year, but the summer months are very hot, with low humidity making the valley ideal for diverse agriculture. Fruit and nut trees thrive, as do vineyards and a wide variety of row crops and cotton fields; the valley helps feed and clothe the whole country. Modesto is almost in the middle of this vast flat area, and Highway 99 connects the largest of the valley towns.

California, either permanent residents or visitors. My first task was to select fabrics that featured printed images of people. As I worked on the quilt, the news of the day was filled with preparations for a Papal visit to California. I reflected on the visit of the Pope (see story on page 101), and the concept of traveling by chartered buses to visit this famous dignitary. Perhaps the faces in my quilt belong to those people who ride mass transportation, such as the Greyhound® Bus. The question is, who would you see on that bus, maybe the Pope, or just extraordinary people?

On the road again, if you are traveling from Modesto to Los Angeles along Highway 99, there are many small valley towns where the weary traveler can stop for food or drink. If traveling on the newest Interstate Highway 5, the places to stop are rather barren roadside convenience stops with only gasoline and limited food available. Driving along the older highway is more scenic and offers the opportunity to visit the small towns, which seems more civilized than speeding along the fast-paced interstate.

*The Tale of Genji* by Murasaki Shikibu (see reference on page 44) portrays the journeys of Genji as he travels through tenth-century Japan. The next quilt in my travel series includes three pictures reminiscent of Japanese travelers resting after a journey. The pen-and-ink drawn panels are surrounded with colorful patchwork. The border of *The Odyssey Continues, Resting At Tulare* is hand-painted in the style of *Taking The Greyhound To Bakersfield*.

**The Odyssey Continues,
Resting At Tulare**, 40" x 80",
1987

The third quilt in my travel series honors Modesto. "Water, Wealth, Contentment, Health—Modesto" is the statement that adorns the archway in downtown Modesto. The arch was built in 1912. It spans I Street at 9th Street and the words are outlined with electric light bulbs so the message is readable at night. When making this quilt in 1987, I did not know that it was the 75th anniversary of the arch. My quilt is intended to honor those four words that symbolize the gifts found in Modesto: water, wealth, contentment, and health. Each piece of fabric was chosen to convey a personal memory. If traveling north from Fresno on Highway 99, Modesto is the third town along the way that begins with the letter "M." On my travels around the world, I meet many people who have made the pilgrimage to Yosemite National Park, and they often mention they drove through Modesto on the way. The number 3 in the quilt is a reminder that visitors could have traveled through Madera, Merced, or Modesto to approach the west entrance gates to the park.

*Water, Wealth, Contentment, Health—Modesto, 92" x 64", 1987,* gift of Peggy Mensinger to Modesto Centre Plaza

Left: The backing features a drawing of the arch as it spans I Street.

**On The W.E. Brownie Brown,**
**65" x 71", 1987**

In California we have a practice of naming the freeways. I am not sure just how this came about, but quite often when driving along, you will notice a large road sign proclaiming to be the "so and so" freeway. Much of my driving was solo and it was very entertaining to contemplate just who "so and so" might be, or why that name adorns a stretch of highway. I have never researched this custom, instead I named a travel quilt *On The W.E. Brownie Brown*. You may see this sign on Highway 580 South, just after leaving the Altamont Pass area. If you follow the signs toward Fresno 580 South, Modesto next exit, look for the W. E. Brownie Brown Freeway sign on the right hand side of the road before reaching Patterson Pass Road.

In 1988 I had a teaching assignment in San Diego, where two of our adult children happened to be living at the time. The occasion warranted a trip for my husband and me to stay extra days in order to visit with them. The time of year was Mother's Day, and on Sunday we decided to visit the famous San Diego Zoo. Our two sons were enjoying the camaraderie of the event when it occurred to me that most families we saw that day were taking Mother to the zoo. Many of the families had small children in tow, but we had our two grown sons. The quilt made after that trip was both a reminder of the day, as well as an acknowledgment that some of the zoo animals were mothers, too.

What I have learned is that inspiration can be found anywhere—in your hometown or on the pages of the local newspaper. Something sparks the idea that is stored in the creative memory bank. Another event might be the catalyst to bring the memory alive and be transformed into form, like seeing a replica of Lady Liberty in Modesto, where the photograph on page 106 was taken. Perhaps Liberty escaped New York Harbor and found her way to California, a very large state with mountains, seashore, populous cities, suburbia, and agriculture—just like many other states and

*Mother's Day at the Zoo,*
*77 ¹/₂" x 55", 1988*

countries. Angel Island, situated in the middle of the San Francisco Bay, is not well known by tourists, who are interested in the more famous island in the bay, Alcatraz.

In 1988, a newspaper article stated that the wild animal population on little Angel Island was increasing dramatically, and officials decided that something needed to be done because food supplies were limited. In my collection of fabrics was a handkerchief with a printed map of San Francisco (including the Bay), Statue of Liberty fabric, California Dancing Raisin® fabric, and Mickey Mouse fabric. What if the Statue of Liberty went on vacation to California and decided to stay on Angel Island? What did she see on her trip (a purple dog) that provoked her to want to become a Californian? The answers are in *California Postcard: Having a wonderful time, send money, Love, Libby*.

In 1987, the Museum of Modern Art in San Francisco hosted a traveling exhibition entitled "Tokyo: Form and Spirit" that originated in 1986 at the Walker Art Center in Minneapolis, Minnesota. I had been to Japan in 1986, and seeing this exhibition the following year, along with the gift shop with all the Japanese items, sparked the inspiration to make a two-sided quilt entitled, *This Is A Long Distance Call*. One event I wanted to participate in while in Japan was Kabuki Theater, but my itinerary did not coincide with the scheduled performances. I was fortunate to find fabric featuring famous Kabuki actors in San Francisco's Japantown. The quilt features a theatrical format, with colors and fabrics chosen to replicate stage and curtain. The three central images are hand drawn on white fabric and although not Japanese, they relate to the idea that with a mask, the wearer can portray another identity to the viewer. Side two of the quilt is more specific in dialogue, with the maps of Japan, the Samurai and the Geisha, and calligraphy fabric. The year the quilt was made is the Year of the Hare in the Oriental calendar.

**California Postcard: Having a wonderful time, send money, Love, Libby, 62" x 47", 1988**

**Lady Liberty in Modesto**

**This Is A Long Distance Call,**
**56" x 53", 1987**

Left: The back side of *This Is A Long Distance Call*

*Heavenly Days In Angels Camp*, 45" x 65", 1995, collection of Quilts, Inc.

After we purchased our soon-to-be retirement home in the Sierra Nevada mountains, we made the drive from Modesto to Arnold after work every Friday evening. Each trip took us through Angels Camp, which is an 1850s gold-mining town in the Mother Lode area of California. Most people say that Angels Camp is as close to heaven as you can get; it is above the valley smog, the winter weather is mild, and every year the town honors the "Jumping Frog" of Calaveras County that was immortalized by Mark Twain. Many of the businesses in Angels Camp feature the frog image, and the local high school team is known as the Bullfrogs. In May, during the annual frog jump, the town celebrates with a festival. This event attracts people from all over California who bring their frogs to challenge the farthest jump. If Sunbonnet Sue lived in Angels Camp, do you think she would have wings? Is Angels Camp the place where angels camp? Is it always heavenly in Angels Camp?

Farther east, just a few miles away from Angels Camp, is Murphys, another gold rush town. Every St. Patrick's Day the town celebrates with a festival, which includes painting a large green shamrock in the middle of Main Street. Both gold-rush towns have churches with the name St. Patrick's, and Murphys has a wonderful old cemetery adjacent to the church. Part of settling into our new environment necessitated my visiting the local cemetery to visit the permanent residents. There I found beautiful old headstones engraved with the names of Irish and Italian immigrants. I wanted to commemorate this celebration of the green and discovery of special places by combining the Arnold figure (representative of the move to Arnold) with the purple dog—sort of the new image with the old.

*Arnold Meets The Purple Dog,*
*46" x 64", 1995*

## 9

Price 25 Cents

Crowning
the May Queen

BY
ELIZABETH F. GUPTILL.

A SPECTACULAR PLAY FOR CHILDREN

BEST

MANY THINGS INSPIRE ME—COLOR, TEXTURE, NATURE, FLOWERS, AND pretty things all placed in a row. Since a very early age, I can remember how much I liked to look at decorative objects. A favorite admonition of my mother was, "Look but don't touch." One of my favorite hobbies is visiting antique shops, where the first order is to look at all the objects. Especially appealing are items shown in glass display cases; this is where the small treasures lie, and I would not want to miss looking at a single one. Fortunately, some of the treasures that belonged to my family have been trusted to my care.

A picture of ancestors in Croatia, circa 1890, includes my maternal grandmother's mother (standing far left), her parents (seated), and her husband (standing far right). The child in the front is Aunt Mary, sister to my grandmother. Another photograph shows siblings standing in front of a calla lily bed in Watsonville, California. My mother (third from left) with her twin brother are both dressed in gingham shirts and pants. Interesting to note that a photograph of my father's family shows my father (seated in the middle), wearing a dress.

Quilting was not a family activity, so there are no quilt heirlooms. I have purchased many antique quilts that served as inspiration for my work, and a few of the very special quilts that were once in my collection have been donated to museums. Although I have never made a traditional quilt, the designs appeal to me.

Memories are part of the family experience. When I was young, memories were not something to dwell on; life was spent living and building events for future reflection. Only later in my life, now that I am old enough to remember the losses, does memory play an integral part in my creative life. I have made a few quilts specifically as memory quilts. In 1987, my friend Steve Kalar set out to take images found in my baby book and transfer them onto fabric. We chose old pictures of my parents as well as other images, up to the day of my wedding. The fabrics chosen to surround the transferred images were selected because they conveyed a feeling of the time— from my parents' meeting to the day of my wedding. The set of the quilt and the top border suggests looking through a window. The large floral print and the faded blue star fabric were both curtain fabrics from the period and are used to frame the pictures in the quilt.

*In Loving Memory, 83" x 90",*
*1987*

1. **Detail of Rainbow Round the World quilt, circa 1928.**

2. **Detail of silk Log Cabin quilt, circa 1880.**

3. **Detail of old textile. Crazy pieced lap robe with "squibbling" technique, date unknown.**

4. **Detail of cotton Nine Patch variation with U.S. Grant fabric.**

5. **Nine Patch variation with U.S. Grant fabric, circa 1860-1880;** quilt in the collection of the Los Angeles County Museum of Art, Los Angeles, California.

6. **This circa 1880 Log Cabin style quilt is the first that I purchased for my collection.**

7. **Detail of Prairie Point block, circa 1930.**

8. **Detail of Silk Victorian Throw, circa 1880, inspiration for the feathered kimono,** *Diamonds on Ice.*

9. **Detail of Amish "Hole in the Barn Door," hand-dyed cottons, circa 1875.**

*Memories of Childhood,*
58" x 53", 1988

When I was in Catholic school, on the first of May we had a festival where everyone participated; each age group had a specific role. A procession honored Mary, the Virgin Mother, and flowers were a big part of the event. The youngest children carried baskets full of rose petals that were dropped, one petal at a time, along the path. The older high school girls carried cut flowers wrapped in sheaves that they held in their arms as they proceeded toward a statue where empty vases awaited. Finally, one special chosen girl carried a crown made from flowers. When she approached the statue, she placed the crown on the head of the Virgin Mary. All the while, the participants sang a special song: "Oh Mary we crown Thee with blossoms today, Queen of the Angels, Queen of the May."

When I reached the appropriate age for carrying a sheaf of flowers, the chore before the event was to color the calla lilies. The nuns, who were our teachers, were not content with plain white calla lilies; we had to crush pastel colored chalk into a fine powder to use as the coloring agent. And fine it had to be, no lumps. If lumps were visible, you were encouraged—sometimes with a ruler tap on the shoulder—to try again, to roll a glass jar over the chalk that was spread on wax paper, carefully, so as not to tear the paper, or you would have a real mess. The powder would then be dusted onto the calla lilies, the excess was shaken off, and magic—pink, blue, yellow, orange, and lavender calla lilies. I guess the coloring made them more heavenly. At the time, I could not help think that if God had wanted colored calla lilies he certainly would have provided them. Now, so many years later, I see colored calla lilies in the local nursery; they have been hybridized, but not in time for when I needed them.

Many of my quilts and wearables are made using colorful fabrics that I have purchased. Since 1981, when I began to hand paint my own fabrics, I have made quilts or garments that feature a softer coloration. Instructions and samples for painting silk fabrics are included in my 1994 book, *Colors Changing Hue*. I continue to work alternating between pastel and bright colored pieces. When I wrote *Six Color World* in 1997, hand painting fabrics was again the theme, using a brighter array of colors in combination with purchased fabrics. Also included in that book are techniques for other surface embellishments, such as overpainting gold on black fabric.

Through the years, a well-known functional object, the teapot, has become a prized decorative art object. I enjoy looking at illustrations of special teapots, especially in books that feature collections of the wacky, obviously nonfunctional, as well as the most beautiful teapots. These unique works of art are inspiring because they turn an ordinary item into something extraordinary. In 1996 I set out to make a teapot quilt. The design was based on one of my drawings that I thought was successful. When I tried to translate the drawing into a quilt, my efforts weren't as successful as I had hoped. Fortunately, I had not begun to stitch it together. I put it up on my design wall where I could look at it. After a few weeks, I took the piece down and took it apart. To make the design work, I had to forget the drawing and let the teapot tell a story; from there the whole concept took shape.

For almost ten years, I have tried to make an annual trek to the cemeteries of Colma, California, to photograph the variety of elaborate statuary. My last trip sparked the title for my teapot quilt. At the edge of a rather large monument to one family, names were inscribed of those buried beneath. Violet Maud was a Victorian woman. This is her story quilt.

*Violet Maud, Rapture, and Tea*, 59" x 37 ¹/₂", 1996

## 10

Yvonne Porcella '96

HOLLYWOOD

# in the
# shade
# of
# spring
# leaves

I BEGAN TO PAINT SILK FABRICS BECAUSE I WANTED A SPECIFIC COLOR AND pattern on fabric; Marble Fudge ice cream, slightly melted, and stirred. This sounds like a strange reason, but I was interested in creating a unique fabric without the difficulty of vat dyeing. My experience with fabric dyeing began when I was a weaver. I would hand dye my own yarns, often using natural dyes (see *Colors of Nature*, page 17). I also over-dyed ethnic textiles when needed for a specific outfit. If ribbon designs or the embroidery were the wrong color for a garment, I often over-dyed them with synthetic dyes. My friend Maggie Brosnan was a fiber art teacher, and she would often hand dye fabrics for me during her class demonstrations. I would purchase a fifty-yard bolt of silk, and when there was extra dye in the pot, Maggie would throw in a yard or two for my use.

Eventually it became necessary for me to color my own fabrics (by this time Maggie could no longer create the special fabrics), and I was not interested in synthetic dyes. Coincidentally, around the same time I was asked by a local shop if I would like to test a new imported fabric paint. I invited two friends to my studio, and together we tried every possible technique. *Six Color World* includes some of those experiments tested almost twenty years ago.

**Cynthia, 1995 (pattern from Colors Changing Hue),** hand-painted silks decorate the doll, collection of Cynthia Kukla

**Floating World, 76" x 66", 1982.** Shown in *Quilt National '83*, toured France and Turkey in *Quilts Contemporaines Americanes*, 1984-86, collection of the artist

***Wisteria le deuxieme*, 42" x 36",
1995.** Shown in *Diversity! Art
Quilts for The Next Century,* collection of the artist

1. ***Tide Pool, vest, 1997***

2. ***Garden Bouquet (detail)***

3. ***Love Lingers Where The Water Flows, 61" x 49", 1988,*** private collection

4. ***Blue Champagne,*** vest with hand-painted silks and burned silk appliqué

5. ***A World Beyond the Clouds, haori coat, 1981.*** Shown in *Quilt National '81*, private collection

6. ***Tide Pool (detail)***

7. ***Evergreen, wallhanging, 10' x 6', 1993,*** collection of Dr. & Mrs. Jerry Jones

Because I use textile paint that is pigment suspended in an acrylic base, care needs to be taken to avoid stiffening the fabric. I was interested in painting silk, yet I wanted to retain the natural supple quality; the answer was to dilute the paint with water. Most of my silk fabric colors are pastel, very much like a watercolor painting. I enjoy using this palette as an alternative to my bright and colorful commercial fabric quilts and garments. Perhaps the inspiration comes from our living among the almond trees.

When working with hand-painted fabric, I begin by coloring the fabric, using a variety of techniques on different types of fabric, then I design the quilt. Sometimes I have to paint additional colors to make the piece complete. I find that using different subtle textures in the same quilt often gives the piece depth.

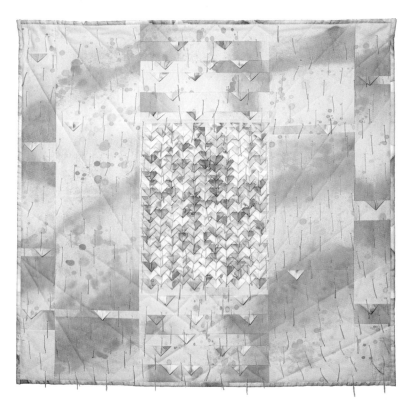

*Morning Mist,* **50 ¹/₂" x 47", 1984,** collection of Roy Young; Fairfield Processing Corporation

Right: *Sundancer 684,* **58" x 62", 1984,** private collection

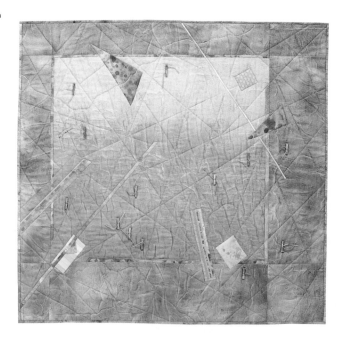

***Diamonds on Ice, 60" x 48",
1984,*** feather kimono, collection of the Fine Arts Museums
of San Francisco; The M. H. de
Young Memorial Museum

## 11

# LATEST WORK, NEW STUDIO:

THE OPPORTUNITY FOR ME TO HAVE A SMALL STUDIO AROSE WITH OUR move to the mountains. In the past, I was accustomed to working in a larger space that had north-light windows and outdoor access where I could paint my fabrics. In our new home, we converted a carpeted bedroom into my new workspace. Storage cupboards, 8' high by 11' wide, fill the east wall and are used to store fabrics, books, miscellaneous treasures, and photographic records. I put my 4' wide x 8' long x 38 $\frac{1}{2}$" high design table in this 15' x 15' room. With the 24" deep by 27" high table extension that opens on hinges to make space for my sewing machine, the room is pretty crowded. A south wall serves as a design wall and is covered with a 7' x 8' gridded flannel fabric. Track lighting on the east wall above the cupboards gives good light to the design wall; however, I found that the lighting on my table was not conducive for working. For the most part I was working in a shadow.

Eventually we decided to add on a larger studio space that took advantage of the beautiful north view of the forest. The new 15' by 25' room adjoins the old room and is perfect for a studio, but it also is a wonderful addition onto our home. We included an outdoor deck that can be accessed through French doors. Water is available on the deck, and I added a utility sink in the new studio, which is large enough to wash painting equipment and fabrics.

Shortly after moving to the mountain house, I had an accident with a bottle of black textile paint in my studio. One of the cautionary dictums that I proclaim when teaching is that textile paint will also stain porous surfaces in addition to your fabrics. Painted walls, unsealed concrete patio floors, unsealed wood, carpets, kitchen tile grout, etc., are all susceptible to misguided paint. I was a victim of my own words when a bottle of black paint fell off my table and the lid broke, spilling the contents onto the carpet. Of course, it would not come out and simply sank to the padding when I added cleaner, and wicked up into the nap once it dried. For a while, I covered this errant spot with a throw rug until we could replace it with a carpet scrap. My new studio has a beautiful polyurethane sealed pinewood floor that is easy to clean.

I preach that my creativity is not determined by the size of my creative space, but I do think that an artist should be comfortable and work in a pleasing environment. For me, a larger space also offers the room to try new techniques and methods. I thought about renting a larger studio space in town, but security might be a problem and winter access could be difficult. I enjoy working at home, and the only drawback seems to be that I do not hold conventional hours. When the creativity is flowing, working could continue all day and then long into the night.

I moved my big table into the new room, and I have a portable table in the small studio. When working on a project, this second table holds my fabrics so that my large studio table is available for construction. My design wall still fills the south large wall. I can pin work-in-progress to the flannel surface and view it from thirty feet away.

Again, lighting is an important factor in the larger studio. During the day, the north exposure gives wonderful light. At night I wanted something that would eliminate shadows and give natural light. The ceiling is very high, so conventional track lighting would not be close enough to my work. I chose to use track lighting but to extend the fixtures on adjustable cables. The clear glass shades also diffuse

the lighting. Regular light bulbs did not provide excellent night lighting, so I switched to neodymium 100-watt bulbs. At last, the perfect solution. I can turn on three lights to flood my table, two lights over the sewing machine table, or all five lights. Bullet track lights serve the corners of the room, and there is a separate fixture over the sink.

Eventually I will have a pull-down ironing board mounted in the wall, but for now I use a small portable board. I have a metal shelving system to hold my painting supplies near the sink. Quilt storage is currently in the guest bedroom, which is decorated with 1930s era quilts, and in Modesto, it is in my old studio space. Sometime in the future I plan to have shelving built on the west wall to hold rolled quilts.

The northwest corner of the room has developed into a wonderful corner for sipping a cup of tea, having lunch with a friend, or reading books. I decided to do something frivolous and added an antique crystal light fixture over the table.

My business office is still in our Modesto patio home. I find that this works best for me, even though I may not receive the mail every day. Currently I am not ready to move all my archival materials and files to the mountain house. We happen to live in the middle of a forest, and there is always danger of fire during the

**a quiet corner**

**guest bedroom**

**fabric storage**

Right: **bookshelves**

long, hot, dry summer season. Four years ago, a wildfire called for the evacuation of the entire area, and many California Fire Departments made a valiant effort to save affected properties. Keeping my office records in another place seems like a good idea.

Predicting the future is not possible, but I do know that I will continue to work in my new studio and enjoy the possibilities of what my creativity will bring forth. My whole career just seems to have developed, and I have not set any goals for the future. My personal rhythm calls for completion rather than having unfinished projects, so I focus on each individual piece one at a time. Perhaps the fact that I like to finish projects before taking on the next one leads me to the "cross the bridge when I get to it" approach. I remember my mother cautioning me not to "count my chickens before they have hatched" so I never would suppose future success or events. I have had a wonderful journey and hope to continue for many more years.

Like every artist, I have periods of what is called angst; reflection on past work and hesitation about what future work will or should be. At one such moment in my life, I used the questioning period to think about what I wanted to make. As a passenger in our car, I began to notice road signs that sparked a past interest I had in the colorful square or triangular directional signs. I came home and sketched out a stop sign, yield sign, and a sign that showed a circular

bend in the road. The design led to making a quilt which I call *Time Master*, how we use the time we are given to master our skills, pertaining to both work and play.

The world headquarters of the Nabisco® Company in New Jersey includes a gallery where they show a variety of art represented through all media. In 1997, I was asked to submit slides for consideration for the multi-media exhibition, "Inspired by Nabisco..."; artworks that were inspired by any Nabisco product. I went to my local grocery store and walked the aisles looking for the Nabisco trademark red triangle in the upper left

Recently completed quilts include a technique where I first draw a small picture. (See *Success* on page 90 for the first quilt made in this method.) I sketch out an idea and use tracing paper to change the sketch, adding elements if necessary. All the while I am aware of how seams could be constructed in the patchwork or piecing. This technique is like drawing a jig-saw puzzle where each shape fits into the next. After I am satisfied, I trace over it with a black pen and, if necessary, reduce the drawing on a photocopy machine to a six-inch image.

The next step is to put the six-inch drawing onto the glass plate of my art projector so that the image will be transferred to the wall. By moving the projector forward or backward, I can make the image as large or as small as I want. This determines if the six-inch drawing will be suitable for a large or small quilt.

I have a roll of 24"-wide uncoated butcher paper that I tape together, if necessary, to get the large size I want. I begin by pinning it to the flannel design wall. I transfer the drawing to the paper by tracing over the projected lines

*Time Master*, 49" x 53¹/₂", 1996

with a felt-tip pen. Transferring the image to the paper is best done in a darkened room to be able to see the drawn lines. Drawing over the projected lines gives me the opportunity to change curves or proportions. This paper drawing becomes the cartoon. A cartoon is a full-sized preparatory drawing on heavy paper that is used for fresco and mural paintings, tapestries, stained-glass windows, or works of art that require a full-scale reference. Some artists save their cartoons, and with important works of art, the cartoons find their way into museum collections. The cartoon for James

McNeil Whistler's peacocks, painted for *Harmony in Blue and Gold: The Peacock Room* (the room is permanently installed at the Smithsonian's Freer Gallery in Washington, D.C.) was displayed during his retrospective exhibition at the National Gallery of American Art in 1995. After finishing my cartoon, I lay the butcher paper on my large table and cover it with the same-size piece of very thin white cotton fabric, which will become the underlining. With a pencil, I trace the design on the cotton. Next, I begin to select the colors for the quilt. I have the option of tracing

another paper pattern for each individual section if I want, or I can cut directly into the fabric to create the pattern shape.

At any time I could scan the design into my computer to sample colors for each part of the drawing. But for me, this takes away from the spontaneity of the design. I like going to my fabric collection and finding the perfect print and color to fit within my design. I work each section as I go, substituting fabrics and colors as needed. If necessary, I may make a trip to the fabric store to purchase additional fabrics.

After pinning the fabrics in

place, I stitch (either by hand or machine) through the cotton underlining. I find this stabilizes the top that is made up of all the different shapes that are rarely cut on grain. The underlining can be cut away if desired before batting and lining the quilt.

*Biscuits, Triscuits, and Bones*, 41 ¹/₂" x 62", 1997

corner of any box. Although I found many specific items, I decided to make a quilt featuring my purple dog appliqué pattern. Nabisco makes chewy bones for dogs under the trade name Milk-Bone®, as well as cookies, biscuits, and crackers in a variety of shapes for human consumption. I chose to use the shapes of a bone, a biscuit, and a Triscuit®.

In March 1997, I was honored to receive an invitation to exhibit a large piece in the 9th International Triennial of Tapestry at the Central Museum of Textiles in Lódz, Poland. The exhibition would open in May 1998, but the required photography and paperwork were due in the fall of 1997.

When I began to contemplate just what type of quilt I would make I had many ideas, but I wanted this quilt to have special meaning. The approaching end of this century brought many thoughts to my mind before I put them on paper. I reflected on the 1933 *Century of Progress* World's Fair Quilt Exhibition that generated many unique designs. What had we, as Americans, accomplished since then that profoundly affected the world? Following the tradition of tapestry, which tells a story, I tried to distill the many themes of the twentieth century when designing my quilt. I thought about the legendary Johnny Appleseed who wandered the lands throwing out seeds. Could it be that we throw out ideas or "seeds" without consideration of what will take root? In the 1960s, everyone spoke of the power of peace, but with what seriousness? Probably the most important effect of technology this century is the ability to communicate instantly. The internet makes this possible. Most people and countries face the crossroads of development— from agricultural villages to global villages— where open lands become future cities. The world is full of positive and negative things. Have we done it all, or is there more to come? But what single event has changed the way we fight wars as well as offered immense mathematical possibilities? With Einstein's work he leapt forward in mankind's knowledge of its universe. As this century closes we are all consumed with changing the clock and writing the new numerals. I found it interesting that I could take the numeral "2" from the equation "e=mc$^2$" and join it to 2000.

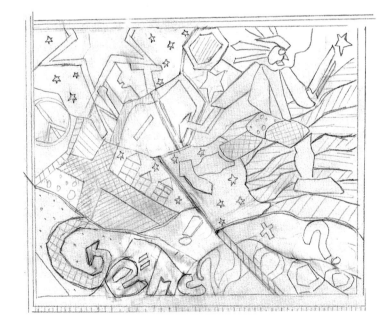

After pondering these thoughts, I began with paper and pencil. I made a small sketch which excited me with possibilities. With a little revision, the design was adjusted to compensate for appropriate seamlines. I enlarged the drawing into a cartoon. The quilt would be approximately nine feet square. This I divided into four manageable sections. I started to construct the quilt top in April and finished the quilt four months later. In the beginning, two days were spent stitching strip-pieced units of color together, which I sewed into stripes and checkerboards.

As the design progressed, I decided to stitch the quilt top by hand. Having worked with tapestry techniques as a weaver, this is the discipline I wanted to

demonstrate in this quilt. There was something that led me to re-create the feeling of laying in the colors by hand, even though the colors here were printed fabrics and not weaving yarns. I used the same technique of laying in colors in 1971 on the tapestry rug I wove for *Better Homes & Gardens*.

Making quilts is a very labor-intensive art form. Spontaneity is difficult because of the nature of the techniques used. Cutting directly into the fabric is one way

to be spontaneous, and many artists are using that method. I find that I like some control, probably due to the fact that I am spending so much time on making a quilt. With some art forms, such as oil painting, you can over-paint or even scrape off paint. Today, fabrics are getting more expensive to buy, and making random cuts could be considered frivolous. In the quilt *Success* on page 90, I did random cut some of the appliqué designs. I wanted irregular edges instead of smooth curved edges. With scissors, I cut the shapes out of the fabrics and then did hand appliqué. I have also used this random cutting method in making machine embellished wallhangings. In *Still Life With Five Oranges*, on page 54, some of the leaf, the orange, and the flower shapes are designed by simply cutting into the fabrics.

*Answering the Riddle,*
*102" x 110 1/2", 1997*

**Garden Party, vest**

I also used this technique of cutting shapes when I designed my 1998 Fairfield Fashion Show garment, and I returned to the theme of a still life. For the vest, I began with irregularly cut background colors and fused them to an underlining. Then I made flowers by cutting shapes freehand out of fabric. With the flower shapes in hand, I began to make my "garden" on the front and sides of the vest, and then finally, the vase with flowers on the back. The vest design was constructed as a flat shape with button closure on the shoulders. This offers the opportunity to open out the vest and enjoy the flow of colors and shapes from the left to right fronts.

During the gray gloomy days of January, I was struck with the feeling of how easy it would be to become depressed during such cold and snowy times. My husband and I had recently traveled to Santa Barbara, where the weather was glorious and sunny. Bright blue skies and flowers every-where—only in Southern California! I threw open the doors to my fabric storage and pulled out red fabric. The result was a machine appliquéd still-life quilt. I began with a classic urn shape, filled it with flowers, and surrounded it with a border of vines and leaves. It was a colorful response to winter. See page 138 for an image of this quilt and pages 2 and 3 for a detail.

This book represents a period of my career of more than thirty years. Although there are many more creations in my repertoire, the limits of this volume prevent me from being tempted to include more. I have dabbled with oil painting, doll making, knitting, sewing, and writing, and we can all be happy that I have not chosen to take up the performing arts. I did enjoy singing with my school choir; fortunately that features a blend of voices where mine could be hidden.

**Marilyn Wright shares her daughter's quilt.**

I thought it might be interesting to present here a photograph taken upon the occasion of my birthday in 1996. In the beginning of this book, I mentioned that fortunately there is no record of the first quilt that I made in 1963. I did make another quilt for a godchild, Kathy Wright, during those early years. As I was still not fluent in the techniques of patchwork, I decided instead to quilt three layers of fabric together. My choice was a white pique cotton with a blue and green scattered floral motif. I used black thread and hand quilted around each of the printed elements on the fabric. At my birthday party, Marilyn Wright, mother of Kathy, brought the quilt to share with me. It was truly a poignant moment for me.

*Crimson Delight,*
42 $^3/_4$" x 58", 1998

*An Amish Adventure: 2nd Edition*, Roberta Horton

*Anatomy of a Doll: The Fabric Sculptor's Handbook*,
    Susanna Oroyan

*Appliqué 12 Easy Ways!* Elly Sienkiewicz

*Art & Inspirations: Ruth B. McDowell*, Ruth B. McDowell

*The Art of Silk Ribbon Embroidery*, Judith Baker Montano

*The Artful Ribbon*, Candace Kling

*Baltimore Beauties and Beyond (Volume I)*, Elly Sienkiewicz

*Basic Seminole Patchwork*, Cheryl Greider Bradkin

*Beyond the Horizon: Small Landscape Appliqué*,
    Valerie Hearder

*Buttonhole Stitch Appliqué*, Jean Wells

*A Colorful Book*, Yvonne Porcella

*Colors Changing Hue*, Yvonne Porcella

*Crazy Quilt Handbook*, Judith Montano

Crazy Quilt Odyssey, Judith Montano

*Crazy with Cotton*, Diana Leone

*Curves in Motion: Quilt Designs & Techniques*, Judy B. Dales

*Deidre Scherer: Work in Fabric & Thread*, Deidre Scherer

*Dimensional Appliqué: Baskets, Blooms & Baltimore Borders*,
    Elly Sienkiewicz

*Easy Pieces: Creative Color Play with Two Simple Blocks*,
    Margaret Miller

*Elegant Stitches: An Illustrated Stitch Guide & Source Book of
    Inspiration*, Judith Baker Montano

*Enduring Grace: Quilts from the Shelburne Museum Collection*,
    Celia Y. Oliver

*Everything Flowers: Quilts from the Garden*, Jean and Valori Wells

*The Fabric Makes the Quilt*, Roberta Horton

*Faces & Places: Images in Appliqué*, Charlotte Warr Andersen

*Fantastic Figures: Ideas & Techniques Using the New Clays*,
    Susanna Oroyan

*Focus on Features: Life-like Portrayals in Appliqué*,
    Charlotte Warr Andersen

*Forever Yours, Wedding Quilts, Clothing & Keepsakes*,
    Amy Barickman

*Fractured Landscape Quilts*, Katie Pasquini Masopust

*Free Stuff for Quilters on the Internet*, Judy Heim and
    Gloria Hansen

*From Fiber to Fabric: The Essential Guide to Quiltmaking
    Textiles*, Harriet Hargrave

*Hand Quilting with Alex Anderson: Six Projects for Hand
    Quilters*, Alex Anderson

*Heirloom Machine Quilting, Third Edition*, Harriet Hargrave

*Imagery on Fabric, Second Edition*, Jean Ray Laury

*Impressionist Palette*, Gai Perry

*Impressionist Quilts*, Gai Perry

*Jacobean Rhapsodies: Composing with 28 Appliqué Designs*,
    Pat Campbell and Mimi Ayars

*Judith B. Montano: Art & Inspirations*, Judith B. Montano

*Kaleidoscopes & Quilts*, Paula Nadelstern

*Mariner's Compass Quilts*, New Directions, Judy Mathieson

*Mastering Machine Appliqué*, Harriet Hargrave

*Michael James: Art & Inspirations*, Michael James

*The New Sampler Quilt*, Diana Leone

*On the Surface: Thread Embellishment & Fabric
Manipulation*, Wendy Hill

*Papercuts and Plenty, Vol. III of Baltimore Beauties and Beyond*,
    Elly Sienkiewicz

*Patchwork Persuasion: Fascinating Quilts from
Traditional Designs*, Joen Wolfrom

*Patchwork Quilts Made Easy*, Jean Wells (co-published with
    Rodale Press, Inc.)

*Pattern Play*, Doreen Speckmann

*Pieced Clothing Variations*, Yvonne Porcella

*Pieces of an American Quilt*, Patty McCormick

*Piecing: Expanding the Basics*, Ruth B. McDowell

*Plaids & Stripes: The Use of Directional Fabrics in Quilts*,
    Roberta Horton

*Quilts for Fabric Lovers*, Alex Anderson

*Quilts from the Civil War: Nine Projects, Historical Notes,
Diary Entries*, Barbara Brackman

*Quilts, Quilts, and More Quilts!* Diana McClun and Laura Nownes

*Recollections*, Judith Baker Montano

*RIVA: If Ya Wanna Look Good Honey, Your Feet Gotta Hurt . . .*,
    Ruth Reynolds

*Say It with Quilts*, Diana McClun and Laura Nownes

*Scrap Quilts: The Art of Making Do*, Roberta Horton

*Simply Stars: Quilts that Sparkle*, Alex Anderson

*Six Color World: Color, Cloth, Quilts & Wearables*, Yvonne Porcella

*Small Scale Quiltmaking: Precision, Proportion, and Detail*,
    Sally Collins

*Soft-Edge Piecing,* Jinny Beyer

*Start Quilting with Alex Anderson: Six Projects for First-Time
    Quilters*, Alex Anderson

*Stripes in Quilts,* Mary Mashuta

*Tradition with a Twist: Variations on Your Favorite Quilts*,
Blanche Young and Dalene Young Stone

*Trapunto by Machine*, Hari Walner

*The Visual Dance: Creating Spectacular Quilts*, Joen Wolfrom

*Wildflowers: Designs for Appliqué & Quilting*, Carol Armstrong

*Willowood: Further Adventures in Buttonhole Stitch Appliqué*,
    Jean Wells

For more information write for a free catalog:
    **C&T Publishing, Inc.**
    **P.O. Box 1456**
    **Lafayette, CA 94549**
    **(800) 284-1114**
    **http://www.ctpub.com**
    **e-mail: ctinfo@ctpub.com**

For quilting supplies:
    **Cotton Patch Mail Order**
    **3405 Hall Lane, Dept. CTB**
    **Lafayette, CA 94549**
    **e-mail: cottonpa@aol.com**
    **(800) 835-4418**
    **(510) 283-7883**

Five

ETHNIC
PATTERNS
Yvonne Porcella

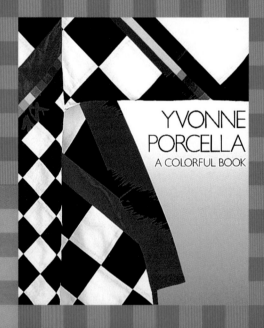

Plus Five

Ethnic Patterns
Yvonne Porcella

# PIECED CLOTHING

Yvonne Porcella

Pieced Clothing

VARIATIONS

Yvonne Porcella

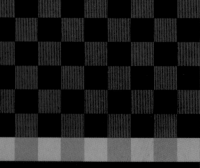

YVONNE PORCELLA
sixcolorworld

COLOR · CLOTH · QUILTS & WEARABLES

YVONNE
PORCELLA
A COLORFUL BOOK

YVONNE
COLORS CHANGING HUE
PORCELLA